GUNS, KITES AND HORSES

GUNS, KITES AND HORSES

Three Diaries from the Western Front

Edited by Sydney Giffard

[signature: Sydney Giffard]

The Radcliffe Press

LONDON • NEW YORK

Published in 2003 by The Radcliffe Press
6 Salem Road, London W2 4BU

In the United States and in Canada
distributed by Palgrave Macmillan, a division of St Martin's Press
175 Fifth Avenue, New York NY 10010

ISBN 1–86064–906–8

A full CIP record for this book is available from the British Library
A full CIP record for this book is available from the Library of Congress

Library of Congress Catalog card: available

Royalties arising from sales of this book will benefit the
Royal Artillery Institute, Greenwich

Typeset in Sabon by Oxford Publishing Services, Oxford
Printed and bound in Great Britain by MPG Books Ltd, Bodmin

Contents

List of Illustrations

Some Acronyms and Abbreviations

'A'	A Battery
A 91	A Battery, 91st Brigade
A/75	A Battery, 75th Brigade
A/76	A Battery, 76th Brigade, and so on, with B, C and D: standard Battery/Brigade designation
ADS	advanced dressing station
AG	advanced gun
Amm/ammu/amu	ammunition
Anzac	Australian and New Zealand Army Corps
Archie	anti-aircraft guns and gunfire
arty	artillery
AVC	Army Veterinary Corps
'B'	B Battery
BAC	Brigade Ammunition Column
Bart.	Baronet
Batt/btty/Bty	battery
BC	battery commander
Bde/bdg/Bgde/Bge/ Brg/Brig.	brigade
Bdr/Br.	Bombardier
BEF	British Expeditionary Force

BGRA	Brigadier-General Royal Artillery
BHQ	Brigade Headquarters
BMRA	Brigade Major Royal Artillery
Bn/Btln.	battalion
BSM	Battery Sergeant-Major
'C'	C Battery
C de G	Croix de Guerre
C Gds	Coldstream Guards
CCS	Casualty Clearing Station
CDQ	prearranged call for fire
CG	Coldstream Guards
Clm	column
Cmd	Command
CO	Commanding Officer
Col	Colonel
Coy/Co	company
Cpl	Corporal
CRA	Commander Royal Artillery
'D'	D Battery
DA	Divisional Artillery
DG/DGs	Dragoon Guards
Div	Division
DSO	Distinguished Service Order
Dvr	Driver
E and Y hut	a sort of predecessor of the NAAFI
FA	Field Ambulance
FOO	Forward Observation Officer
FWL	Forward Wagon Line
G Gds/GGs	Grenadier Guards
G–D	Grand Dogger
GDA	Guards Division Artillery
GOC	General Officer Commanding
GOCRA	General Officer Commanding Royal Artillery
GOC-in-C	General Officer Commanding-in-Chief

Gr(s)	Gunner(s)
GS	General Staff
H/Huss.	Hussars
HB	Howitzer Battery
HEs	high-explosive shells
How (Gn. How)	howitzer (German howitzer)
HV	high velocity
IG/I Gds	Irish Guards
K	Lord Kitchener
KBS	Kite Balloon Section
KDG	King's Dragoon Guards
KSLI	King's Shropshire Light Infantry
L/Lancs	Lancashires
L Gds	Life Guards
Lincs	Lincolnshire Regiment
MC	Military Cross
MG	machine-gun
MM	Military Medal
MO	Medical Officer
NAAFI	Navy, Army, Air Force Institute
NCO	non-commissioned officer
NSW	New South Wales
OC	Officer Commanding
OM	Old Marlburian
OO	Orderly Officer
OP	observation post
PMC	President of the Mess Committee
QMS	Quartermaster Sergeant
RA	Royal Artillery
RAMC	Royal Army Medical Corps
RB	Rifle Brigade
RF	Royal Fusiliers
RFA	Royal Field Artillery
RFC	Royal Flying Corps
RHA	Royal Horse Artillery

rly	railway
RN	Royal Navy
RO	Recording Officer
RTO	Railway Transport Officer
RUSI	Royal United Services Institution
S Gds/SGs	Scots Guards
S-M	Sergeant Major
S/S	Staff Sergeant
Sgt	Sergeant
SLI	Somerset Light Infantry
sub	subaltern, or subsection (gun and crew)
Toc H	Talbot House
VAD	Voluntary Aid Detachment
VC	Victoria Cross
WL	wagon line
WO	War Office
X	section usually of two guns from battery
Y Day	countdown to zero day when attack began
YMCA	Young Men's Christian Association
Z	zero

Foreword by
Professor Richard Holmes

One product of the current popularity of history is interest in primary sources that might not have seen daylight half a century ago. How many sets of 'great-uncle's old papers' were once thrust back into an old suitcase or consigned to the skip when the family moved house? Now any historian working on the First World War cannot but be struck by the remarkable flowering of its archives, perhaps most notably in the collections of the Department of Documents at the Imperial War Museum and the Liddle Archive at the University of Leeds. But there are some accounts that are too valuable to lie in big brown boxes, picked over by scholars: they deserve exposure to a much wider audience.

The Giffard papers are undoubtedly a case in point. They consist of the diaries of three of the sons of Rycroft and Cecy Giffard of Lockeridge House near Marlborough. One, Jack, was a regular gunner officer, badly wounded when L Battery Royal Horse Artillery attained immortality at Néry on 1 September 1914. The battery, surprised by close-range fire while watering its horses, got two guns into action: three VCs were awarded to those manning one. The other gun, Jack's, was knocked out early on, its detachment all killed or wounded. Another son, Eddie, was managing a sheep station in Australia when war broke out, but returned to England and was commissioned into the Royal Artillery. He went to France in November 1915 and remained on the Western Front throughout the war, rising to command a battery: he was killed just before the war ended, and his last diary entry reports rumours of an armistice. Walter Giffard had lost the lower part of a leg as the result of a shooting accident, but managed to become a balloon observer, and plied his dangerous trade at Ypres during the last year of the war. This was only part of the family's contribution to the army. Jack's twin brother Bob was mortally wounded on 31 October 1914 when German shells struck Hooge château, housing the staffs of the First and Second Divisions. Another brother, Sydney, was killed at Gallipoli.

The Giffard papers underline truths easily forgotten in our very different age. Upper middle-class families like the Giffards, their roots earthed firmly in the Victorian era, had a strength and commitment that helped temper the mainspring of national resolve. Rycroft Giffard lost three of his boys in the war. But, as Sydney Giffard (who has edited his family papers so well) rightly observes: 'Grief removed neither the conviction that the war had to be fought and won nor the sense of pride in the contribution to the achievement of victory.' Although Jack was too badly injured to fight again, he stayed in the army throughout the war, and Walter, who could so easily have avoided military service altogether, chose to risk his life in a kite balloon, declining a safe job, as 'I do not think it is playing the game.' But he had no doubt that it was a dangerous one. 'The Hun burnt five balloons immediately to the north of us today,' he wrote in May 1918. 'The old blighter, not content with burning the balloons followed the observers down in their parachutes firing at them.' Yet there is no sense of jingoism in these diaries, no feeling of hatred for the Germans: just an unshakable commitment.

Nor is there any sense of an army burning with mistrust of its high command and seething with incipient mutiny. It is easy to judge the Western Front by its poetry or literature. However, many combatants put up with danger and privation with a tolerance that we find hard to understand, and which often surprised contemporaries looking back through the prism of the 1930s. In these diaries there is none of that disillusionment that characterized so much reflection on the war: the moment brought its own concerns and rewards. 'We had a room in a cottage and excellent straw beds in a barn,' wrote Jack of his last night before being crippled. On 24 March 1918, in the middle of the great German offensive, Eddie Giffard reported laconically: 'Bosche appears to have got through down South: Peronne lost: had a good sleep.' And in April 1918 Walter Giffard, safely down after an ascent with a Canadian who smoked in proximity to the balloon's inflammable gas, happily recorded that he had been awarded his 'wings'. Of course the Giffards had an officer's view of the war. But their landscape was peopled with soldiers, like Gunner Pitt, Jack's servant, killed in August 1914, Bombardier Clarke of Eddie's battery, wounded in October 1916, and Sergeant Whithers, who broke a leg parachuting in March 1918. The Giffards speak to us with the quiet, authentic voice of the Western Front, without that dramatic volume that booms out from some subsequent accounts. We would do well to listen to them.

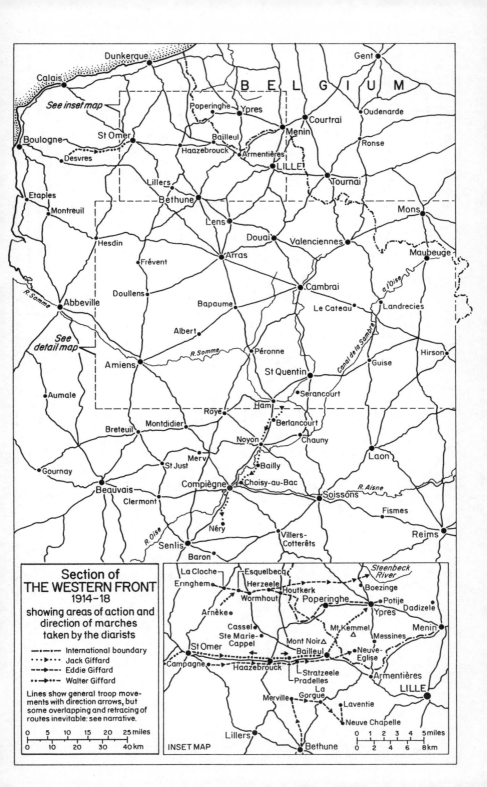

Section of
THE WESTERN FRONT
1914–18

showing areas of action and
direction of marches
taken by the diarists

—·—·—·— International boundary
······▸···· Jack Giffard
–––▸––– Eddie Giffard
••••▸•••• Walter Giffard

Lines show general troop move-
ments with direction arrows, but
some overlapping and retracing of
routes inevitable: see narrative.

0   5   10   15   20   25 miles
0   10   20   30   40 km

0   1   2   3   4   5 miles
0   2   4   6   8 km

INSET MAP

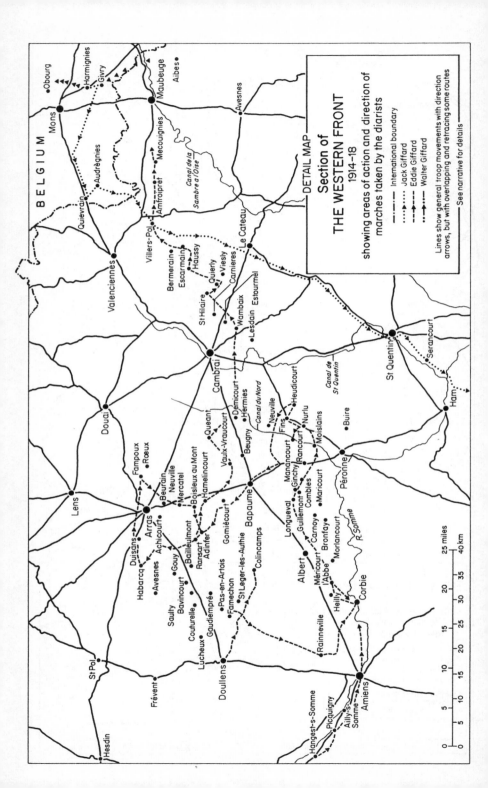

1

Introduction

Jack Giffard

Lieutenant Jack Giffard was carried on board SS *Lydia* at Le Havre, bound for Southampton, exactly one month after embarking at Southampton with his battery on SS *Rowanmore*, bound for Boulogne on 16 August 1914. His diary gives a continuous narrative of his experiences during that month. More than ten days of it were spent in the fighting retreat from Mons, and just over two weeks in beginning his recovery from severe wounds received in the action on 1 September on account of which the battery is still known as L (Néry) Battery, Royal Horse Artillery.

The improvised dressing station to which Jack and others were taken from Néry fell into German hands for some days. The diary and a few other small valuables were kept hidden in the rafters above Jack's bed whenever there was a danger of inspection during those days. He brought the diary back to England with him and his sister Maud later copied it out for their father, H. R. Giffard (known in the family as Dad, Dud or Rycroft), at Lockeridge House. After Dad's death in 1934, this copy of the diary was taken to the nearby house in which Maud subsequently lived with her sister Polly; there it remained in the attic for the next 50 years, together with Jack's brother Eddie's original diary also now reproduced below. It is unclear what Jack did with his original diary. He may well have made it available to the War Office, but he would have considered it unlikely to be of general interest and would certainly not have wished it to attract attention to himself.

Lockeridge House in the 1920s.

Maud's handwriting was not unlike Jack's, but the condition of the copy she made is such that it could not have gone through Jack's ordeal. It is, however, self-evidently a complete copy. One or two mistakes were made in the copying. For example, although Jack's spelling of proper names may not have been invariably correct, he would not have misspelled his battery commander's name (the only curiosity it has seemed necessary to correct in this presentation of the text). Maud was no doubt also responsible for a puzzle found near the beginning of the diary, the solution of which serves to bring out the character of the diary as a whole.

On 18 August, the third day of his battery's active service in the British Expeditionary Force and their first full day in

France, when Jack is extremely busy as orderly officer, he finds time to remark on the sudden death of 'Jimmy Greison'. This must originally have referred to General Sir James Grierson, and it is so interpreted in dealing with that day's entry, in the notes that follow the diary below.

Jack Giffard dressed to ride to hounds, seemingly just across the road from Lockeridge House.

It is not only the correct identification itself that is of interest, however. Grierson actually died in a train near Amiens on his way to Sir John French's headquarters on a visit preliminary to his assuming command of II Corps. In her book *The Guns of August* Barbara Tuchman observes that 'among the British [Grierson] had been the closest student of German military theory and practice.' His death was a serious loss to the BEF, with whose commander-in-chief he had been on terms of close friendship. One consequence was that the command of II Corps was given to Sir Horace Smith-Dorrien.

The differences that arose later between French and Smith-Dorrien were not apparent during the retreat from Mons, when the latter earned his C-in-C's formal commendation. The point here is that Jack Giffard was fully aware of the significance of Grierson's death. He noted it, but did not need to explain. There are many similar notes in Jack's diary. In observation, as in action, he is keen and alert. The diary is part of the business in hand. It is intended to provide material from which it may be possible to draw useful conclusions later. Meanwhile, there is no time for expansion or reflection while on active service. (After Néry there will be other constraints, but it is remarkable how sharply focused the observation remains in spite of them.)

During the earliest days of the retreat and the artillery battle around Le Cateau, Jack managed to retain and record a number of immediate impressions from which there were clearly tactical lessons to be drawn. On 24 August he noted that the battery had 'got off about 400 rounds' and done 'considerable execution amongst the infantry'. This confirmed that the Royal Horse Artillery's quick firing 13-pounder, with its shrapnel shells timed to burst low over the target, was a most effective weapon against infantry massed in the open. The narrative brings out the speed, mobility and flexibility of which a crack battery was capable, as well as the striking power of its six guns. But the cost is also noted and 'we were most extraordinarily lucky'. The implication of this day's account is that the horse artillery was more skillfully employed than the cavalry. L Battery 'enabled what was left of the cavalry to withdraw' and 'retired with the remnants of the cavalry', the brigade having 'suffered very severely'. A charge by the 9th Lancers and two troops of the 4th Dragoon Guards, covered by L Battery, was especially expensive. Jack does not comment directly, but he may have wished to remind himself to question that particular move when the time was appropriate for critical reflection. His silence on the work of the British infantry,

A review, perhaps at Larkhill, presumably with L Battery in review order.

notably the Norfolks and the Cheshires, in this action may be taken as confirmation of its excellence.

On 26 August Jack recorded that 'we saw an English battery wiped out by lyddite' (perhaps 11th Battery, Royal Field Artillery) and that 'the Germans opened on our ridge with big high explosive shell.' He was evidently already aware that, especially when it came to counter-battery work, the almost complete reliance of the British artillery in the field on shrapnel as opposed to high explosive shell would need to be corrected. This proved to be one of the most important changes brought about as the result of the experiences of the BEF in the retreat from Mons.

The diary shows well how, despite losses (including the comparatively minor inconvenience of having been parted temporarily from their baggage), extreme fatigue from lack of sleep and the difficulty of covering great distances on heavily congested roads, L Battery remained a coherent fighting unit capable of going into action whenever this was required of them: and covering the retreat of slower and less flexible elements of the BEF was a role to which the RHA were of course recognized as being uniquely well adapted.

Their guns could fire up to 20 rounds a minute to a maximum range of about 6500 yards, and then vanish.

A battery of horse gunners in 1914 would normally have five officers and about 90 other ranks. Each of its six guns, usually, as in L Battery, 13-pounders (sometimes 18-pounders) would have its limber, carrying 24 rounds of ammunition, gun and limber to be drawn by a team of six horses. There would be 12 battery wagons with their draught horses, which would include in their contents some 150 more rounds of ammunition per gun, as well as all the impedimenta needed on active service. The battery, with one other, would also be supported by the brigade ammunition column, with at least as many shells available for replenishment as were carried by the batteries themselves. The number of draught and riding horses with a battery would be well over 200. Although everyone went short during the retreat in 1914, the arrangements for provisioning and supply of the original BEF were up to the standard of the exceptional fighting proficiency of all arms.

After the rigours of the long retreat it is good to read how Jack was still able to enjoy the luxury, for one night, of the house on the Aisne at Choisy au Bac. Then there was the night at Néry and the terrible action in the misty dawn. The diary raises the question of whose fault it was that they were taken by surprise. This is still much discussed and there is no simple answer. Accounts of the action itself do not differ sigificantly one from another, but Jack's diary though inevitably incomplete has an immediate authority. He allows himself one despairing cry about 'all that remained of what three weeks ago left Aldershot the finest horse artillery battery in the world'. For the rest, he reports the facts as he observed them during and after the fight. He notes the times of moves, the number of cases in the dressing station and of those looking after them, and lists his surviving belongings.

The time spent at Baron in the improvised dressing station for all that Warrington, the RAMC officer in charge, and his fellow Territorial orderlies could do must have been grimmer than the diary admits. The park itself, outside, was no doubt as pleasant as it remained when visited 80 years later. But Jack's ordeal, the suffering and death surrounding him, the uncertainty of the outcome, whether in terms of health or of destination, and the frustrating inability to communicate with home were enough to test the hardiest of spirits. With the help at first of morphia, the diary, despite its having to record some sad events and to contemplate briefly the possibility of prolonged captivity, remains remarkably cheerful. The German captors are regarded with a balanced good humour, allowed on occasion to be correct, even considerate, but recognized as 'dirty dogs' at other times when their behaviour falls below acceptable standards.

Beyond his preoccupation with the local situation, which develops as a series of minor skirmishes, Jack notes signs that Marshal Joffre's strategy may be working. His anxiety about his own condition is related primarily to the possibility of getting on the move again. He is always grateful for what is done to help him by the doctor and his orderlies, and by talented scroungers. Conscious of the need to build up his strength he gets what enjoyment he can from food and wine, especially after the slaughter of the delectable porker. But he sits up in a chair for the first time, 'very weak and groggy', only the day before he and his closest fellow convalescents, Butler of the Life Guards and Renton of the King's Dragoon Guards, who was with the Queen's Bays when he was wounded at Néry, arrange their ramshackle but effective departure from Baron. This is contrived largely by the 'redoubtable' Hopkins, a memorably stout and resourceful character deservedly given a hero's role in the diary, whose subsequent career, however, lies unfortunately like all the others beyond the limits of Jack Giffard's narrative.

Jack's surprise and pleasure on finding that Dad has come to meet him at Le Havre, bringing a trained nurse and 'every conceivable sort of thing' he could possibly have wanted from his wife and accelerating his onward journey to hospital in London, bring the diary's narrative towards its conclusion. Jack and Margaret Long had been married in Bradford on Avon only in January 1914. The first of their four daughters was born in February 1915. Before that and before Jack was fit enough to return to duty even at a desk his twin brother Bob was among the casualties, with other members of General Lomax's staff of the First Division, in the first battle of Ypres in the critical phase of the fighting round Gheluvelt on 31 October, dying of his wounds the following day.

The twins, born in 1884, had been very close in the family, at school, in the army class at Marlborough and in the Shop at Woolwich. Their army careers then diverged, the one winning his jacket as a horse gunner, the other developing a different expertise as an inspector of artillery and then, with the outbreak of war, on the staff. Bob had married four years before Jack: his widow is mentioned in Walter Giffard's diary and their daughter Robina in Eddie's. Both twins were keen regular soldiers when professional standards in the British Army were as high as they have ever been in peacetime. Jack was also a keen cricketer, playing for I. Zingari in the immediately prewar summers after a tour of duty under Lord Methuen's command in South Africa. (Photographs of Jack's survive showing the C-in-C seated with erstwhile enemy Boer commanders in an atmosphere of reconciliation.) He was a good shot. Above many other accomplishments useful to an Edwardian army officer he was a fine horseman, entitled to regard his days out with the Beaufort Hunt as an essential part of his continuous training. He took a serious rider's interest in the horses he rode and that worked with him and his battery. The diary shows that the slaughter of the horses at Néry affected him deeply. After all, he would probably have reckoned, soldiers elected to expose themselves to risk but Harriet and Sealskin were given no choice.

His wounds had been so serious (they caused him pain for the rest of his life) that Jack was never to be passed fit for active service again after Néry. He returned to duty first at the War Office and at Woolwich. After Bob's death the family was hit again by the news that Sydney Giffard had been killed in action on Gallipoli at the very beginning of May 1915. Jack obtained an account from a brother officer, an extract from which is given in the Appendix below, together with Sydney's last hastily pencilled note home, evidently written within hours of his becoming a casualty, in which he asks for reinforcements of his favourite tobacco.

Jack, who had been honoured by the French as a Chevalier of the Légion d'Honneur in recognition of his gallantry during the retreat and at Néry, was rapidly promoted Major. He was then selected to join the British War Missions to the United States. As a Brevet Lieutenant-Colonel he served on the Anglo–Russian subcommittee arranging for purchase by the British government, through Messrs J. P. Morgan and Company for the Russian government, of large quantities of munitions and other material and their shipment to Russia. When Brigadier General W. Ellershaw returned to England to accompany Lord Kitchener on his projected visit to Russia, and was lost with him in HMS *Hampshire*, Jack was left in charge of this work. He remained in the United States until the work was wound up, and was appointed OBE in recognition of his services there. His second daughter was born in New York, the event noted in Eddie Giffard's diary.

Although he was invalided out of the army a few years after the war, Jack was still able to ride and he competed with success in show jumping at the Olympia international horse show. Knowing all about horses but wholly innocent of chemistry, he was briefly involved with the ill-fated Yadil company. But the desirability of a warmer climate to reduce the persistent pain of his old wounds led him to Southern Rhodesia where he settled to grow tobacco on Mlembwe Farm, Banket, and where his four daughters grew up in peace. He was on good terms with successive governors, most particularly with Sir Godfrey Huggins. He was a Justice of the Peace and for many years presided over the Salisbury race club, polo club and horse show.

He made occasional visits to England, coming back to Lockeridge about the time of his father's death in 1934 and once after the Second World War. A photograph survives, taken during this last visit, of a family group outside the Ailesbury Arms in Marlborough where they had gone for the annual mop fair. He died aged 72 in 1956. His obituary in the *Marlborough Times* included the following summary by his brother Walter: 'Jack was blessed with good looks, a kind and generous nature, and made a host of friends.' Walter's note briefly outlined the career of an elder brother for whom he retained a deep affection, evident in correspondence that survived them both. The note also remarked that, keen as Jack Giffard was on his army career, 'he enjoyed to the full the Edwardian hey-day as he continued training for the deluge.' Although very grim events are recorded in the diary, it may nevertheless also succeed in communicating to the reader a capacity to enjoy life that was pretty nearly inextinguishable.

Eddie Giffard

Major Edmund Hamilton Giffard had the satisfaction of entering in his diary a note that forecast the armistice, but he was to die of his wounds shortly before hostilities ended. He had lived through three full years of active service on the Western Front and the shell that killed him was one of the last to fall near his battery. The battery's last round of the war was fired at the enemy while Eddie was still in command.

Eddie Giffard's diary presents no problems other than, occasionally, of legibility, the pencil's mark having faded in some places. The diary is contained in five pocket-sized notebooks, the first one opening upwards (as opposed to sideways) and held together by an elastic band, the others all T. J. and J. Smith's 'automatic self-registering pocket note-book'. This title signified that 'on the pencil being inserted it is securely retained [by a small metal clip, now mostly rusted away, once fitted into the cloth binding] in a convenient position, clearly indicating the leaf to be next used'. The last of these notebooks is fitted into a black leather wallet whose end pocket holds a photograph of Eddie's niece, Robina Giffard, aged about six with a spaniel by her side. This may well have been taken at Lockeridge House, to judge by the clump of pampas grass in the background. (Clumps of pampas grass at intervals along the so-called Marlborough Walk survived at least until the mid-1930s.) Some of the notebooks also contain operational jottings: map references, lines of fire, distances to targets, unit designations, brief draft messages and so on. None has retained its pencil.

Eddie, born in 1887, was the fourth of the six sons and the seventh of the 11 children of H. R. (Rycroft) and C. M. (Cecy) Giffard. He followed the twins, Bob and Jack, at Horris Hill Preparatory School and at Marlborough College, into the army class but not into the army. He went out to New South Wales to take part in the operation and management of the sheep station at Collaroy, which had been founded and developed by his mother's Hamilton family. It seems likely that he had spent some time learning the business at the London end first. He remarks in the diary in the winter of 1915 that it is five years since he last saw snow. This suggests that he did not go to Australia until two or three years after leaving school. At Marlborough he was a keen games player and steady all-rounder. When Siegfried Sassoon went to Lockeridge House to play cricket for his Marlborough College House against H. R. Giffard's XI, it would have been at Eddie's invitation since they were near contemporaries: but there is no evidence of their having kept in touch.

Presumably, Eddie left Australia on or soon after the outbreak of war in order to volunteer his services in England and to catch up with his three regular gunner brothers. Before he was fully trained, not only had Jack been knocked out at Néry but also his brothers Bob and Sydney had both been killed at Ypres and in Gallipoli respectively. It seems likely that he had hankered a bit after the peacetime style of his brothers from whom he may also have absorbed much useful advice. However that may be, he evidently assumed the role of artillery officer quite easily. It seems to have suited him quite apart from the desire to emulate his brothers and to do his best for the country's cause. In this he simply shared the motivation common to the great majority of his generation. One of his friends, who wrote later of Eddie's outstanding example of 'willing endurance' (a phrase that seems particularly apt), also remarked that, although a wartime soldier only, he had the professionalism of a regular.

His diary is a bare record of his daily preoccupations at the front, when resting, or in reserve. The periods of home leave are omitted. What matter are the weather, the conditions for men, horses and equipment, and the day's work. Occasionally, there is no time to make any note at all or the days slip indistinguishably past. Events in other sectors or on other fronts are mentioned only when they seem of such importance as to have affected the strategic balance, and sometimes rather casually at that, as in the entry for 6 February 1917: 'America breaks off Dip relations with Germany: very cold wind.' As to the final outcome of the war,

King George V and Queen Mary (possibly still Prince and Princess of Wales) with general officers and officers of the Royal Horse Artillery and others.

no hint of doubt can be detected. There is no sign of the philosopher, still less of the pontiff, in the simplest possible account of a (mostly) junior officer's experience of the Great War at its most hideous. Though Eddie seldom comments on the morale of those around him and never questions the durable strength of their determination, he does show a constant awareness of what the chaplains may be able to contribute to its sustaining. His own religious faith is very evidently strong.

The many complex technicalities of gunnery do not feature in Eddie's diary. He does not even specify the equipment of any of the batteries with which he serves, but no doubt it was usually the famous 18-pounder gun on which the Royal Field Artillery principally relied throughout the war and sometimes the 4.5-inch howitzer. While some, including the 61st Brigade, RFA, with which he served for a time, were all-howitzer brigades when the original BEF went to France in 1914, the standard organization by about the time Eddie reached the front was for A, B and C batteries in an RFA brigade to be equipped with six 18-pounders each, and for D Battery to have six 4.5-inch howitzers.

For many years visitors to the Imperial War Museum in London, once inside the main hall, found themselves facing side by side a 13-pounder gun as used by the Royal Horse Artillery in 1914–18 and an 18-pounder as used by the Royal Field Artillery. The latter type fired over 99 million rounds from British Army batteries in France and Belgium during the Great War, being by far the most extensively used British artillery weapon. Expertly handled the 18-pounder could fire up to 20 rounds a minute, but at such a high rate of fire the gun would soon deteriorate, while it would remain in good condition if limited generally to four or five rounds a minute in action. Its maximum range, which was much the same for the 13-pounder and the 4.5-inch howitzer, was 6500 yards. It was deployed in close support of the infantry, even at times effectively in the front-line, and also on counter-battery work. Eddie's diary sometimes notes the number of rounds fired by battery or section, where high rates are sustained, and he once mentions that the battery is only some 800 yards from the German trenches. In more normal circumstances, at longer ranges, he records on two or three occasions that the barrage, or creeping barrage laid down by the guns, has exactly met the requirements of the infantry. Close liaison with the infantry was always essential and a gunner acting as forward observation officer would get to know the frontline very well.

Field guns can be manhandled over short distances, but supply and mobility were dependent on horses. Each gun and limber, and every wagon, had its team of six horses,

14

reduced to four in many cases towards the end of the war, of necessity but at the expense of efficiency. Horses brought up supplies of every requirement, including replenishments of ammunition, quantities of both high explosive and shrapnel shells. If wagons could not get through the mud, packhorses and mules had to do so. The peacetime complement of a field artillery brigade was about 200 riding horses and 550 draught horses. Casualties were heavy and the care, management, supply and replacements of horses was a constant preoccupation when resting or in reserve no less than when in the line. Notes of concern over the availability of water for the horses are more liable to be treated in the diary as crises than are any of the other circumstances of war.

The attainment of increasing accuracy in carrying out ever more complex fire plans put very taxing demands on the gunners. The conditions in which they had to perform their tasks tended to worsen, the mud getting deeper every winter, the enemy's counter-battery techniques developing with their own. Only in the last few months was there easier movement into country that, as Eddie notes, had retained some of the elements of civilized life. But even in the summer of 1918 life was made harder by a virulent outbreak of flu, forerunner of the devastating postwar scourge. Sickness reduced detachments temporarily and it was not uncommon for three men to have to do the work of twelve. Eddie himself was clearly in less than robust health from about the time when he achieved the height of his military ambition with the command of 'A' Battery, 75th Brigade.

With the technical evolution of the artillery, organization at battery and brigade level had become steadily more sophisticated, manpower requirements more demanding. At the end of hostilities the last wartime commanding officer of the 75th Brigade, Royal Field Artillery, Lieutenant-Colonel T. Kirkland, DSO, produced (no doubt at his own expense) a roll of honour covering the period from 24 August 1918, when he assumed command, until the armistice on 11 November. In addition to those killed in action and died of wounds, it listed all battle casualties and included some overall detail. It gave the average fighting strength of the brigade in those months, in total for all ranks, as 634. This was made up of 28 officers, 135 NCOs and artificers, 261 gunners and 210 drivers. The total number of casualties in all ranks during the same period is 214, of whom 20 were killed in action or died of wounds, while 194 were wounded, including 25 listed as gassed. The date and place of every casualty is given. There is also a complete roll of officers. Brigade headquarters was not large, so the average daily strength of each battery will have been little less than the brigade's total divided by four. The number of casualties in 'A' Battery was the lowest. Some of those listed can be related to entries in the diary. It is encouraging to find that a good few of those named in Eddie's brief chronicle were among the survivors.

Captain J. G. Waddell, who had been Eddie's second in command, took over from him and commanded the battery during its march into Germany. He was in touch with the family at Lockeridge House and later brought them the casing of the last shell fired by A Battery, still under Eddie's command, before the armistice. Others who wrote to his father about Eddie included Captain Okell, the Church of England chaplain to 75th Brigade, RFA; and the senior chaplain to the forces, with the Guards Division, F. W. Head, MC, both of whom referred to Eddie's unfailing helpfulness to them in their own work; and various brother officers, among whom Major Foley produced the phrase already quoted of 'willing endurance'. His qualities of leadership and his kindliness and comradely spirit were amply attested from men who served under him as well from his superiors and peers.

In his three years on the Western Front Eddie Giffard was often on the move, so he became familiar with most of the British Army's sector between Ypres and the Somme. He served throughout in batteries and brigades that formed part of the Guards Division Artillery, acting mostly though not invariably in support of infantry battalions of the Guards Division. He joined 'D' Battery of 76th Brigade, Royal Field Artillery, in November 1915 near Neuve Chapelle. He was at once absorbed into the routine of an essentially defensive period, holding a line in low, wet ground near the River Lys overlooked by the enemy on the ridges to the east. There was no break in

The garden at Lockeridge House.

the battery's work, which included some local moves of position, until his first ten days' home leave in early February 1916.

On return from his first leave Eddie found that the battery had had to move back some 200 yards, 'OP all knocked out.' They were relieved a few days later for rest and training before moving to Ypres in mid-March. Apart from the odd spell in the wagon line, there was little respite from the firing line in the salient until Eddie's second home leave in early May 1916. The battery's designation was changed from D/76 to 'C' Battery, 61st Brigade, in mid-May when they went back for a period of 'the usual "rest" routine, ... stables, exercise, etc.' before returning to Ypres a month later. There are gaps in the diary about this time, whether due to the hard monotony of training or to the exigences of the firing line. News of the British offensive on the Somme is slow to reach them in the salient and the diary for 7 July 1916 notes only that it 'does not seem to have got on quite so well the last two days'.

At the end of July the brigade is sent south to 'very nice country like Salisbury Plain' on the River Authie west of the Ancre. They are relieved in late August and arrive on the Somme at the beginning of September for the last and most successful phase of the offensive of 1916. Here they take part in the heaviest fighting (with one day out for a 'joy ride' to Amiens in the general's car) until Eddie gets a week's rest at Mericourt in November. Conditions towards the end of the Somme battle of 1916 were probably as grim as they got anywhere at any time. The artillery barrage was sometimes creeping forward at no more than 25 yards a minute, as this was the best pace the infantry could manage in the deep mud. The gunners were constantly in action under tremendous strain. The rest at Mericourt, with a visit to the cathedral in Amiens and tea sometimes in the charming village of Heilly (was its grand house still occupied then?), must have come as a great relief. Soon after this the 61st Brigade is dissolved and Eddie goes to 'B' Battery, 75th Brigade, RFA, and then to his third home leave. He is now a lieutenant and has earned a warm commendation from the CO of the 7th Lincolns for his work as a forward observation officer with that battalion on the Somme.

Eddie's new battery is back in the line in early December 1916 and there is some feeling that those who have been so recently in the Somme battle are inadequately rested. The mud is 'appalling'. Eddie is given the impression that he may be appointed ADC at 74th Brigade, but nothing comes of it. He is awarded his Croix de Guerre avec palme and is promoted acting Captain. The Germans begin to draw back but it is 'bad pursuing weather'. The brigade comes out of the line at the end of March 1917 and Eddie joins 'A' Battery.

They are given some rest after their prolonged and sustained effort on the Somme, at first in reserve behind the same sector then, in mid-May, near St Omer. Then they are off to Ypres again and are detached to support the Anzacs at Messines. Eddie helps to put out a fire ignited by shells falling on the mobile wagon line shortly before the massive preliminary bombardment on 3 June for the big 'push' on 7 June. They are then transferred to the northern section of the Ypres salient. Eddie is sick, perhaps from food poisoning. Friends help him to avoid being sent to hospital pending the arrival of the warrant for his fourth home leave on 19 June 1917.

Soon after returning to France on 8 July and rejoining the battery in the salient Eddie has a spell commanding it in action. When Major Hovil comes back from temporary duty in charge at brigade headquarters, Eddie relinquishes command of 'A' with regret. Heavy fighting continues in the third battle of Ypres and, on 21 September, Eddie receives a 'blighty' wound in the head, having noted in his diary for the previous day that 'we go out to rest on 22nd.' Colonel Bethell, commanding 75th Brigade, 'very kindly said that he would try and keep my place for me'. Bethell later writes to confirm this adding, 'I greatly appreciate the way in which you commanded and kept A/75 together under very trying conditions.'

Eddie got back from hospital at the beginning of December 1917 to find the brigade once again on the Somme. He joined 'C'. They moved in the middle of the month to camp near Arras, when Eddie seems to have had another spell in command of 'A'. They are back in the line in the same sector in early January 1918 and later that month Eddie is sent on a battery commanders' course in

England. Soon after he rejoins the brigade, in the last week of February, there is expectation of the great 'Bosch' offensive (Eddie, sparing with the vocabulary of rancour, never masters the spelling of Boche, and is not good at proper names either). On 21 March the offensive hits their sector. There is heavy fighting round Arras into the summer, though things seem easier, and there is talk of various allied successes by the time Eddie goes on his fifth home leave in early August.

When he returns there is clearly a strong forward momentum, which is maintained, but it is always a costly advance. After a short bout of flu Eddie takes over command of 'A' Battery in October. He is wounded a few days later but is able to resume work after four or five days under the doctors' care. In early November he has what seems like a bout of flu but keeps going with difficulty. He catches up with the advancing battery on 7 November. The entry for that day says 'Quiet night and good rest after all.' The following morning the diary notes rumours of armistice; and Eddie is fatally hit.

As remarked above, his diary gives a very sparse or terse account of Eddie's war. But the reader who keeps in mind the circumstances in which it was compiled, who is aware what conditions were like on the Western Front, with seas of mud in a devastated landscape, constant shellfire and a permanent concentration of all the other horrors of modern warfare, will find that it has much to add between its lines, not least about the character of the diarist and his comrades and about their view of the Great War. They seem to have seen it essentially as a job to be done with maximum efficiency and minimum fuss. It has been fashionable at times to question whether such a view was ever anything other than a pious myth, comforting and face-saving but still a myth. It is diaries such as Eddie's and other first-hand accounts that keep history in touch with reality.

Walter Giffard

Walter Ernest, born in 1896, was the youngest of the 11 children of H. R. and C. M. Giffard. His first name had a long ancestral resonance; the second was probably chosen as a compliment to Ernie Maurice, one of 11 brothers of the famous Marlborough family, two of whom were soon to marry Walter's two eldest sisters. Walter followed his own brothers Bob and Jack, Eddie and Sydney to Horris Hill and Marlborough College (Henry, the eldest, having chosen the direct route into the Royal Navy). He was a talented games player, especially at cricket and hockey, but he suffered a shooting accident when he was 16 by tripping over brambles in the West Woods, simultaneously pushing off the safety-catch and pulling the trigger as he stumbled and discharging his shotgun into his left leg. His sister Polly, who was with him, was fortunately sufficiently well up in first aid to be able to apply a tourniquet. His left leg had to be amputated just below the knee. The operation was performed on the kitchen table at Lockeridge House by his brother-in-law Walter Maurice. He used to relate that as he came round from the anaesthetic he was conscious of Walter Maurice's voice saying, in the hope of comforting him, that it should still prove possible to get him into the Yeomanry. He thought it best not to reply that the Yeomanry had no major place in his ambition.

While convalescing Walter Giffard became an accomplished bird photographer, acquiring the patience to wait and watch in silence and without movement. He was keen on Richard Kearton's books and never lost his interest in birds.

He was 18 years old when war broke out in 1914. His disability seemed at first to rule out his acceptability as a recruit. He went to the agricultural college at Wye, but persisted in his application to be considered fit for active service. While at Wye he was often invited to shoot or play tennis with the Loudon family at Olantigh and there was ample proof of his recovery. With the help of the artificial leg provided by the renowned establishment at Roehampton, he became remarkably agile.

It was while playing tennis at Olantigh that Walter heard what was subsequently identified as the far distant reverberation of the explosion of his brother-in-law Tom Maurice's ship, destroyed at Sheerness with the loss of all hands by enemy action in May 1915. His brothers Bob and Sydney had already died of wounds received in action, the latter most recently in Gallipoli. Walter always retained a great admiration for each of his brothers' characters and achievements, but Sydney was the closest to him in affection as he had been in age. (While watching a film earlier in that same May Walter had experienced a sudden sense of disaster, so strong that he had felt compelled to walk out of the cinema. He later concluded that this had happened almost exactly at the time of Sydney's death. It was not the only such experience in his life.)

Walter was eventually accepted in 1917 for training in the Royal Flying Corps as an observer in balloons. This offered a satisfactory connection with the business of his gunner brothers. On completion of the training course, which included practice in parachuting, he was posted to join the Second Wing behind Ypres towards the end of 1917. His diary, neatly written in two small nondescript notebooks, was found in a desk drawer after his death in 1971. In the second notebook, started on his return to the front from home leave, coincidentally at the moment of crisis following the launch of the great German offensive in the spring of 1918, he explains that he is continuing to keep his record not because of any interest inherent in his own doings but because 'I suppose this is the most colossal battle, both in magnitude and importance, that the world has ever seen.' The diary comes to an end with his going on home leave again in June 1918. There is no further surviving account of his service apart from the letter quoted below in which he reported to Lockeridge House on his visit to his brother Eddie's grave shortly after the armistice. It seems quite probable that he had accepted suggestions, noted in the diary, that he should take on the less exciting ground job of reporting officer, in which case he might have regarded his own experience of the war as having no further claim to noteworthiness. Nothing further seems to be known of his military career than that he was given the acting rank of Captain and that he celebrated the end of hostilities over dinner in Brussels with immense relief but sadly.

Like the majority of his contemporaries, Walter was reticent afterwards about his time at the front, preferring not to recall it. There were a few anecdotes about fellow cadets in training, including one about a friend who, being found unfit to take part in the passing-out parade, nevertheless contrived to give a startlingly lively impersonation of the Duke of Connaught driving up to the saluting base, if in an unlikely vehicle, at an accurately calculated moment sufficiently in advance of the coming into view of the staff car bearing HRH the Field Marshal in his authentic person to cause the maximum confusion, embarrassment, distress and, for his friends, silent entertainment. Walter would also occasionally enjoy relating an account of his first morning in the mess in France, or perhaps it was in the officers' club in Hazebrouck. He had come down to breakfast, conscious of his inexperience, anxious to do the right thing. There was an elderly Major sitting at the head of the dining table with a labrador by his side. Not wishing to risk seeming distant, Walter thought it best to sit down next to the old man. He patted the dog as he did so.

'D'you like dogs, boy?' asked the Major.

'Yes, Sir,' said Walter.

'Then why don't you bloody well get one of your own?'

This story does not feature in the diary but the general

tone, though serious enough when it comes to the business of war, is light. There are touches of professionalism in the accounts of spotting for the gunners, seeking to convince some sceptics among them of the value of this activity; and, for example, when Walter explains to his CO how it is possible to take a reading of the strength of the wind aloft without having to go up there oneself. There is a certain amount of boyish public school snobbishness of a kind in which Walter would not have indulged in later years. But this is balanced by a willingness to take off his tunic and give a hand in moving equipment with a sense of easy comradeship that is apparently regarded as unconventional, even perhaps inappropriate, by one or two of his superior officers.

Without going into technical detail, the diary conveys a vivid impression of life as it was lived in a kite balloon section at the front. The British had abandoned the spherical balloon by about the time Walter was commissioned and had adopted the Drachen (sausage) balloon used also, and from the beginning, by the French. It was filled with hydrogen extracted from huge steel cylinders and operated from the ground by the section's winch team, the winch itself usually mounted in a lorry. (In a very high wind the balloon could pick up winch, lorry and all and disappear.)

The basket slung below the balloon carried one or two observers. Their primary task was to facilitate the gunners' counter-battery fire by spotting the enemy's gun positions, or the flashes of their gunfire, and providing accurate map references to be passed by telephone to our own batteries. They could work, if conditions were right, by night as well as by day. They were the targets of persistent enemy gunfire from the ground and, though defended by machine guns from the section's lines below, were always liable to come under attack from enemy aircraft. It was a rule in the Royal Flying Corps that an observer might not ask to be

hauled down merely because he was attracting the attention of hostile gunners. At night, gunfire from his own side
was an additional hazard to the balloonist who would hear
heavy shells passing in the darkness with the noise of
express trains.

From a height of say 4000 feet above a winch based on
Mont Rouge or Mont Noir, close by Locre (Loker) and just
off the road from Bailleul to Ypres, an observer could see
for miles beyond the British lines in the Ypres salient.
Walter's kite balloon section were ordered to withdraw
from their advantageous position in April 1918, but as soon
as the German offensive had been contained and reversed he
found himself back in the same area, though now in a
different section. By the time he returned from his second
home leave the final allied advance was about to acquire the
momentum that is apparent in the last four or five months
of Eddie Giffard's diary.

After his demobilization, Walter's completion of his
course at Wye led to his joining the Sudan civil service in the
agricultural department. Meanwhile, he met Minna Cotton,
who had come with her two sisters to stay for a time at the
Lacket in Lockeridge. They were married in 1922 and went,
via Venice, to his house at Shendi on the Nile.

There was a military establishment at Shendi where British cavalry regiments were stationed in rotation. Friendships
were made and retained with numerous officers, several of
whom were to be given important commands in the Second
World War.

By the late 1920s, however, Walter decided that his
career in the Sudan, then considered no place for women or
children from England to spend the hottest months, had
better be abandoned in the interests of family life. He
bought a modest farm at Lockeridge and settled there. When
his father died in the mid-1930s Lockeridge House had to be
sold. Like his father, Walter took an active interest in local

affairs. He served as a Justice of the Peace for many years and was for a time chairman of the bench in Marlborough. He was always willing to give his support and to take responsibility in the activities of village, church and school. His sisters remained in the neighbourhood. He kept in close touch with his brothers, once in the mid-1930s going to visit Jack in Southern Rhodesia.

He thought it very wrong that no serious effort was made to oppose Hitler's march into the Rhineland and became increasingly critical not only of policies of appeasement but also of what he saw as shortcomings in defence policy. On the conclusion of the Munich Agreement he resigned his chairmanship of the local branch of the Conservative Association. He formed a lasting admiration for Churchill. When war came Walter made himself available at once for active service, but had to be content with a vigorous contribution to the formation of the Local Defence Volunteers in the district. Later, as a Lieutenant-Colonel, he commanded the 6th Wilts Battalion of the Home Guard. Minna, who came of a military family, had a role in administration and communications, and was involved in plans devised to meet the contingency of invasion. Their daughter Ann had what was known as 'a hush-hush job' in London, during the blitz, and elsewhere. Walter's eldest brother Henry who, as an exceptionally young captain RN, had fallen under the 'Geddes Axe' after the Great War and had pursued a second career as secretary to the Kent County Council, contrived to rejoin the Royal Navy at the age of 60, but was blitzed out of his office as Port Captain in Southampton and again retired.

By the end of the war Walter had come to regard the social policies advocated by the Labour Party as an essential requirement for success in national recovery and reconstruction. Though his admiration for Churchill as prewar realist and wartime leader was undiminished, he voted for Attlee in 1945, to the dismay of some of his more conventional friends in the neighbourhood. The easy prejudices of his Royal Flying Corps diary were ages away in the past.

Walter was devoted to his wife and family in the full meaning of that worn phrase. He had survived the loss of Minna for four wearying years when he died at the age of 75 very shortly before the death of his brother Henry at 90. Walter was also deeply attached to the village and neighbourhood of Lockeridge and to the Wiltshire countryside, especially the Marlborough Downs, and their birds. It was reported that his last words were, 'Saw a buzzard on the Plain the other day.' But his voice was fading and it seems possible that he said bustard, for there would have been a few pairs of bustards there still, in his youth, and their sighting would certainly have rated a conversational mention at any time.

Background

These three diarists came to the Western Front from different directions to take up different tasks. Their approaches to service on the most demanding battlefields of the Great War reflect these differences. Jack Giffard was a regular soldier accustomed to the highest standards of his profession, for whom the conduct of the retreat from Mons, while it provided new lessons, did not represent a wholly new departure from the discipline of years in training. Denied the opportunity of continuing service in the frontline but considering himself lucky to have survived, as so many of his friends in L Battery had not, he concentrated thereafter on making a success of the unfamiliar but important job in Washington for which he was selected. Of the technical transformation effected in the arts of gunnery as the conflict on the Western Front developed, he was obliged to remain an educated observer.

Eddie Giffard, coming to join up as a volunteer straight

from the sheep station at Collaroy in New South Wales, but with some knowledge of an artilleryman's style of soldiering acquired from his three gunner brothers, was trained to understand that the role of the guns in war was changing. He was to take part in its continuous development. These were circumstances in which initiative and the ability to improvise and innovate had to be grafted onto the original pattern of the gunners' art and discipline. He was fortunate to serve in the Guards Division, a formation whose great strength lay partly in its capacity to adjust to any circumstances whatsoever, including, as they did, both hell and high water. In his diary, reticent though it consistently remains, we see him both as forward observation officer and as battery commander, combining great tenacity with an abiding humanity evidently grounded in his religious faith.

Walter Giffard's opportunity to reach the battlefield was brought about by the expansion in 1916 and 1917 of a comparatively underdeveloped branch of military science. Ballooning was almost the only activity at the front for which a wooden leg was not considered a disqualification. He too was able to draw on his brothers' experience, but he had to learn and devise techniques and routines not yet well established either in the service manuals or in the regard of all of the gunners whose work they were designed to facilitate. His diary directly illustrates how effective the combination of accurate observation from the kite balloon with efficient communications could be in getting gunfire onto its target. It also depicts once more that alternation between unavoidable periods of inactivity and bouts of intense concentration, which must have imposed such a constant strain on those engaged in operations in the air.

For all of them the family, especially the family as symbolized by Lockeridge House, was still at the centre of their lives. This was because H. R. Giffard and his wife Cecy had made it so. H. R. G. (Rycroft to older members of the family, Dad or Dud to the young) was the son of Captain H. W. Giffard, Royal Navy, one of the earliest and most senior naval casualties of the Crimean War, and the grandson of Admiral John Giffard. His brother, G. A. Giffard, became an admiral. His mother's brothers were distinguished public servants, both military and civil, and she herself was a person of indomitable spirit whose benign influence lasted through some 50 years of energetic and creative widowhood.

Rycroft Giffard, born in 1850, spent some time abroad after leaving Eton and acquired some experience of engineering and communications before embarking upon a career in the City. He married Cecy Hamilton in 1878. She was the daughter of George Hamilton, captain in the Royal Navy, and of a family as prosperous, successful and well connected as it was, again, devoted to the service of the crown. Rycroft and Cecy lived for a time in Ebury Street, close to his mother's Stephenson family in St George's Square, and to the Hamiltons in Warwick Square. It became their custom to take a house by the sea, sometimes at Sheringham, or in the country for a few weeks' holiday every summer. This was how they first came to Lockeridge House. They were so pleased with it as a temporary retreat that they entered into negotiations to purchase it as their permanent home, together with a few acres round about it. They moved there definitively some time in the mid-1880s. The seventh of their 11 children, Eddie, was the first to be baptized in the country parish in which Lockeridge was the only one of the four constituent villages not to have a church of its own. (The pattern eventually established was for family marriages and funerals to take place at West Overton church and baptisms at Fyfield, the former being the larger, the latter the closer).

Although he continued with some business interests in

London, Rycroft Giffard became increasingly absorbed in country life with his growing family. There were ponies and dogs for the children and he kept two good lawn tennis courts at the house; he also founded, equipped and captained the village cricket team. He commanded L Company of the 2nd Volunteer Battalion, the Wiltshire Regiment, and on his retirement in 1901 the company marched the three miles out to Lockeridge from Marlborough accompanied by the Marlborough town band to present him with a silver rose bowl. As he became more familiar with the life of the wider community in the country his activities expanded. He assumed the chairmanship of a committee of the County Council, was made a Justice of the Peace and presided over the bench at Marlborough for 25 years; he was also chairman of the board of governors of Marlborough Grammar School, honorary secretary of Savernake hospital and of the Marlborough tennis club, and was active in many charitable causes as well as in local politics. Nearer home again he was chairman of the parish council for something like 40 years, was a churchwarden at Fyfield and took a part in the management of village schooling.

Naturally, Rycroft and Cecy's 11 children tended to regard Lockeridge House as the centre not only of the family's life but also of a wider community, almost as it were of life itself. That this life was strongly rooted in the locality was emphasized by the marriages of the two eldest Giffard daughters, in 1901 and 1904, to two of the 11 Maurice brothers of the famous Marlborough family (of the generation of whom it was said that, if laid down end to end, the brothers would stretch from St Peter's to St Mary's all the way along Marlborough High Street). The careers of five of the six Giffard sons at Marlborough College served at the same time to extend the range of Lockeridge House's social connections. By the time of Cecy's death in 1908 these many connections were so strong that their survival, even at a reduced level of vitality, must have seemed assured.

A group photograph of the Lockeridge House family suggests that its general character was Edwardian. There

The family in May 1910. Back row: *Maud, Eddie, Jack, Polly, Bob, Bob's fiancée Jenny.* Front row: *Henry, Cicely Maurice, H. R. Giffard, May, Sydney.* Ground level: *Tom Maurice, Walter.*

were certain shared peculiarities, most obviously marked in habits of speech. They would all have said, for example, of a visitor forced to withdraw from the tennis courts on account of some respiratory difficulty that he or she had gorn orf with a bad corf. They all referred to time spent at Lockeridge as 'when we were a tome'. Marlborough College lent some points of style to the family by contagion to daughters as well as directly to sons, but the same ethos and tradition of preparation for public service was common to school and family.

Despite these common background features, it was also

a world in which individual character was respected, and self-reliance not merely encouraged but almost demanded. Rycroft Giffard was genuinely devoted to his family, but he expected them to make their own careers. He seems to

The family in 1900. Back row: *Cicely, Henry, Jack, Polly, Bob, 'Aunt' (Laura Hamilton, Mrs Giffard's sister).* Front row: *Eddie, H. R. Giffard, Maud, Ella (H. R. Giffard's mother), Walter, C.M.G. (Cecy), Violet.* Ground level: *May, Sydney.*

have considered that a good schooling was sufficient in the way of preparation for the full responsibilities of adult life. It may be that he regarded the universities with some suspicion as places liable to corrupt rather than strengthen the young men exposed to their sophistication and sophistry. Perhaps that does him an injustice. What is certain is that he regarded the navy and the army, good enough for generations of the family, as providing suitable fields of endeavour for the next generation of men. As for the education of young women, a well-organized country house must be the healthiest recipe for it.

In his consideration of international affairs Rycroft Giffard shared the view common at the turn of the century that Great Britain's position and her ability to consolidate all that was good in the empire were threatened by the excessive ambitions of Germany. On the rare occasions when he spoke of such matters in public, that was likely to be among his themes. In this he was no more than representative of majority opinion in the country at that time. His eldest son, Henry, on voyage to the Far East in the most powerful warship of the day, soon after the triple intervention against Japan in 1898, clearly expected at least an armed confrontation with the Kaiser's battleships. In the longer perspective we may see H. R. Giffard's outlook as a sad irony. If he himself had seen things differently, however, the Great War would still have shattered his world and his family. He was brave enough to turn his mind to devising and, with his daughters' help, administering a local scheme for the improvement of pensions for others bereaved by the war. Life went on at Lockeridge, but there was less laughter in the house or from the garden and fewer footfalls crunched the gravel in the yard or on the drive.

Editorial

For an understanding of the tasks and achievements of the British artillery in France and Belgium during the Great War, the volume on *The Western Front 1914–18* in General Sir Martin Farndale's *History of the Royal Regiment of Artillery* is indispensable. For a wider, general survey of battles and battlefields, John Laffin's *Western Front Companion* is always a reliable introductory guide, while Rose Coombs's handbook, *Before Endeavours Fade*, provides much illuminating detail. All who venture onto this territory owe thanks to librarians at the Imperial War Museum and the Public Record Office. Brigadier and Mrs Timbers at the Royal Artillery Institution in the Old Royal

Military Academy, Woolwich, and Colonel Payne in the Badley Library at Larkhill unfailingly made available deeply expert and sympathetic advice. The gunners of the past will not desert either of those places and anyone wanting to know where their mortal remains might lie may turn to the Commonwealth War Graves Commission for the most careful and exact information.

What it was like for the British artilleryman in particular to be there, with plentiful illustrations of horrible authenticity, is most powerfully conveyed in Aubrey Wade's book, *Gunner on the Western Front*. These are the scenes in which Eddie Giffard spent three years, give or take a few short leaves and spells out of the line and in hospital. For Jack Giffard's war, Richard Holmes's *Riding the Retreat* has recently added a fresh and vivid context. For help in putting Walter Giffard's journal into a broader perspective of the same discipline, Goderic Hodges's *Memoirs of an Old Balloonatic* remains invaluable. More generally, there is much understanding to be gained from listening to the voices collected in Lyn MacDonald's deservedly well-known books, which also include further accounts of the fight at Néry.

To speak of the literature of the Great War is to refer to a treasure house whose exhibits are as remarkable for their variety as for their power, and to which valuable additions are likely to be made for many decades yet. Among autobiographical recollections of the war, those of Blunden, Graves and Sassoon have long been regarded as classics. In recent years, imaginative reconstructions, both fictional and factional, have included striking contributions by Sebastian Faulks and Pat Barker, earning praise and prizes.

If Brooke was for some years the most widely known of the war poets, it is the more searching work of Owen, Rosenberg, Edward Thomas and again Sassoon that has come to command sustained critical attention. As already noted, Eddie Giffard, or possibly Sydney, invited Sassoon to Lockeridge (in age he came between the two). Two other Marlburian poets of the wartime generation were C. H. Sorley and Alec de Candole, Walter Giffard's contemporaries at the college. The less well-known writers are often among the most eloquent witnesses. Of the many anthologies of poetry of the Great War, none does such writers fuller justice than Anne Powell's collection in *A Distant Cry*. Her title is taken from lines by a private soldier, E. H. Evans of the Royal Welsh Fusiliers (with whom Sassoon also served during part of his time, but Mrs Powell's selection excludes survivors).

'My muse was a deep cry
And all the ages to come will hear it.'

The three brothers whose diaries follow this introduction had no vocation from the muse. But their reticent voices may also contribute to the fuller understanding of the complex subject of soldiering in the Great War and of how the character of soldiering changed. At the same time they may serve to suggest that, at least for some of those engaged in the conflict, attitudes towards what they came to regard simply as the task in hand may have changed less than is sometimes presumed. As already perhaps indicated, the three were as different one from another as their shared background permitted. In age, there were only three years between Jack and Eddie. Yet Jack seems to belong to the generation of Edwardians, Eddie to that of the Somme. Walter, eight years younger than Eddie, somehow seems to be hinting already at the sad follies of the 1920s from the height of his observation balloon. In truth, we do not know what any of them thought: we know only what they chose to confide to their diaries.

Still, it is legitimate to speculate. It may be that Lockeridge House best symbolized what they had in common.

Symbolized not merely by the image of the house, though it was once described by an eminent novelist in private conversation as the most beautiful house in the south of England, and not merely by its surroundings, though Marlborough and the Marlborough Downs, Silbury Hill and Avebury, Savernake Forest, the Pewsey Vale and Salisbury Plain itself were inseparably connected with the enjoyment of life, but also by some idea of a set of values, which was expressed through the house because of the family and its faith. The idea of keeping the faith was evidently of some consolation to Rycroft Giffard, as shown by his choice of those words from St Paul's second letter to Timothy for the headstones at his sons' graves. Such ideas, perfectly natural at the time, have come to be thought of often as nothing more than ritual shelters for grief constructed during and after the disaster of the Great War to justify what might otherwise seem beyond justification. A reading of the diaries certainly leaves the impression that these values were subscribed to wholeheartedly without a trace of cynicism or artificiality. Some will find this reassuring; others may think it was merely socially correct. That these were robust individuals seems, however, scarcely open to doubt.

The family's general outlook on life had much earlier foundations, but its leading architect at the turn of the century was undoubtedly Rycroft Giffard's mother, Ella, née Stephenson, an unassuming person, kindly and devout, whose strength of character, referred to above, was at the same time remarkable even by Victorian standards. She is always to be found seated in the centre of photographs of the family taken up to the time of her death in 1906. Sixty years before that she had married Captain H. W. Giffard, Royal Navy. On the outbreak of war with Russia she followed him as far as Constantinople. Then, on learning that enemy shore batteries had destroyed his ship after the

Allied fleet's bombardment of Odessa and that he was severely wounded, she sought and obtained permission to visit casualties from HMS *Tiger* in the Russian hospital to which they had been taken. She arrived too late to see her husband alive, but stayed for a time to do what she could for his ship's crew. The exploit has something to say about the standards of the period in civilized circles as well as about her own personality. Her husband's career, especially towards its end, has been studied in their book *Steam, Politics and Patronage: The Transformation of the Royal Navy, 1815–54* by Basil Greenhill and Ann Giffard.

One of Ella's brothers, a General like their father who had been in the Scots Guards and had become Colonel of the Coldstream, received on his retirement from active duty appointment as Constable of the Tower of London. Visits to great uncle Freddie there were popular occasions for Rycroft Giffard's children and may have had some bearing on later choices of career. (There was, however, competition from plain Uncle Freddie, Cecy Giffard's brother, the most admired among fleets of related admirals, Hamiltons, Keppels, Goodenoughs and Towers.) Ella's other brother, William Stephenson, who had been private secretary to Sir Robert Peel, rose to the highest post then open to an official in the Treasury, but this was a solitary civilian role model: the quill pen could not have outclassed all those plumes and pennants, probably not even if Rycroft Giffard had thought more highly than he apparently did of the ancient universities. A memoir of the Stephenson brothers and of their father, together with a collection of great uncle Freddie's letters from the Crimea, China and Egypt, was later edited by William's daughter, Mrs Frank Pownall, and published with the title *At Home and on the Battlefield*. (It was of course always referred to at Lockeridge as *A Tome and …*)

These influences did not, however, lead the young

Giffards in the direction of literary endeavour. Their diaries were strictly for their own private records. None of them was written with publication even remotely in mind, let alone in view. None of these three war diaries contains reflections on the general nature of war or of its impact either on combatants or on civilians. Nor is there any strategic or political argument in them. Jack was too badly wounded for such taxing pursuits, though he did mention Joffre's bottle. Walter was, one suspects, reluctant to contemplate the war's implications or to risk reviving memories of losses already sustained. Eddie was simply too busy: those who wrote about him afterwards stressed his tireless devotion, even when out of the line, to the far from trivial round of stables, inspections, supply and welfare, and to the daily tasks of forward observation or of plotting and carrying out the battery's fire plans when at the front.

Many other surviving diaries include broader themes. Among recent publications, the *Bickersteth Diaries 1914–18* give deeply felt and considered reactions to varieties of experience of that awful war, and reflections on the politics of church and state. The closest they come to these terse and simpler Giffard diaries is in their profound attachment to and strong expression of the Christian faith, which Eddie Giffard in particular often displays, in this proving more articulate than other members of his family rather than different from them. There is another Marlborough connection here in that Geoffrey Bickersteth's work at the college impressed boys who would go to the front, certainly including C. H. Sorley, just as Geoffrey Fisher's is known to have been admired by Sydney Giffard.

In his introduction to the *Bickersteth Diaries*, John Terraine is surely right to insist on the need to keep it in mind that the men of 1914–18 were nineteenth-century men with nineteenth-century ideas, in particular of patriot-

ism and religion. What he has to say (while avoiding attri-
bution of the point to the Bickersteths) about the Great
War's undermining and demoralization of the middle class
in Britain, to use his own terminology, is harder to relate to
the diaries that follow here. Myths, like beliefs, seem to
come in generations. The diary itself, lying in the attic all
these years, was almost certainly not written in order to
advance a thesis, though keeping it may well have helped
to sustain the writer's morale. The concept of demoralization, as applying to any group or community with which
they were associated, would have been alien to our diarists,
while that of the middle class, perhaps also regarded as
somewhat laughable, would probably have carried conno-
tations with city life.

It is true that H. R. Giffard blamed Churchill for what
he regarded as the ill-conceived expedition to the Dardanelles, partly because the son who was perhaps his favourite,
though he tried not to show it, was killed there. It is true
also that he cancelled his subscription to the periodical in
which H. W. Wilson's *History of the Great War* appeared,
on learning of Eddie's death (so that only volumes I–X
were bound and kept in his bookshelves at Lockeridge).
These were expressions of grief. But he knew well that
many other families had suffered even more sadly than his
own and soon turned to the work of helping some of them.
Grief removed neither the conviction that the war had to
be fought and won nor the sense of pride in contributions
to the achievement of victory. This seems to have been the
attitude of the younger generation too, of the diarists
themselves. But we know for certain only what they wrote.

These diaries are perhaps relevant to some other persistent beliefs about the Great War, which if not properly
to be described as myths seem to be no better than half
truths on the most favourable estimation. For instance, it is
often insinuated that there was no understanding on the

Western Front of the possible effects of modern warfare on the soldier's mind. Yet, Eddie writes of a man's suffering from shellshock in 1916 as though it were a familiar affliction to be treated with natural sympathy. Neither he nor Jack reflects any feeling of lack of confidence in his commanders, nor of distance from the brass hats on the staff, though it is sometimes implied that such sentiments were almost universal, among those slogging it out in the line. Similarly, standards of management are often criticized, but it is certainly true that Jack, Bob and Sydney Giffard, as regular soldiers, were trained, as they were also naturally inclined, to look after others, not merely to command them; and neither Eddie nor Walter would have been likely to fail in this. Eddie, indeed, was noted for his unselfish conduct. Letters of condolence are not always free of hyperbole, but the writer who reported of him that he had enjoyed the respect and affection of all ranks, underlining the last two words, was not by way of attesting an imaginary quality.

On such matters the diaries are often eloquently silent, but, if read and interpreted with imagination and without preconceptions, they may still add something to our knowledge and understanding of action in the Great War on the Western Front.

2

Jack Giffard's Diary

Sunday 16 August 1914

Arrived S'hampton 1.0 a.m. with left ½ battery,[1] Sclater-Booth & John Campbell[2] — remainder 1 hr later. Fine. All aboard by 5.0 a.m. Headquarters & ½ ammun$^{\underline{n}}$ Column came next, & 'I' before us.[3] Steamed out (SS *Rowanmore* (1200 tons)) at 7.30 a.m. escorted by a cruiser. Keeping E-along the coast close in.[4] Slept from 6 a.m. to 9 a.m. after a cup of tea etc. breakfast at 9.00 on duty till lunch. Found a deck chair for the afternoon. Horses fit. Anchored off G–D at 8 p.m.

Monday 17 August 1914

Started disembarking at 5 a.m. all clear by 10 a.m.[5] marched three miles to rest camp on a hill, good water, 1 mile off. Rest of ammu Col arrived in the night. Took the horses out for a walk in the afternoon. Went in B– with Bradbury in a fiacre and a free ride out on a tram.[6]

Tuesday 18 August 1914

Watered horses at 7 a.m. Drill orders 9 till 12 p.m. The others went down to the town after lunch. Self 00 tested sights.[7] inspected rifles & revolvers. More troops came in. Jimmy Greison reported to have died suddenly.[8]

Wednesday 19 August 1914

Exercised the horses at 7 a.m. rode Sealskin. Amu Col & 'I' left by 2 p.m. We entrained at 4.30 p.m. all in one train. Awful trouble with the horses in barbarous trucks. Had to throw one of mine out at Amiens. Excellent dinner at Hotel Bristol. Left 8.30 p.m.

20 August 1914

Arrived at Maubeuge at 9 a.m. Detrained watered and fed & had breakfasts. Marched off at 11.30 a.m. No serious damage to horses. Fine & hot. Billeted by ½ batteries in two farms 8 miles out & ½ mile apart very near Aibes. Comfortable. Plentiful supply of eggs, butter & milk.

Lieut. Jack Giffard, c. 1914.

Friday 21 August 1914

Marched at 5.30 a.m. with Cavalry division[9] & 'D' and 'E' to Givry. 12 miles. 7,000 German Cavalry reported on our right front. We went on with 1st Cav Brig.[10] to hold canal crossings from Aborge[11]–Mousset, but did not come into action, went back to bivouacs at Harmignies with the Division. Had an excellent meal in a Cafe. baggage arrived at 9 p.m. All the march we were showered with flowers, cigars, eggs, & all sorts of food.

Saturday, 22 August 1914

Saddled up ready to move at 4 p.m. (*sic*).[12] Marched at 12.00 with 2nd and 4th Cav Brg with orders to go to an area 10 mls. W. of Mons.[13] Just after starting, news came of a strong German advance on Binche & we were hurried back to E. of Harmignies & took up a position of observation near the station to cover the retirement of 1st Cav Bde. Went into action at 2 p.m. saw the first German shell burst at 12.55 p.m.!! Heavy firing on our right till 4 p.m. Greys & 4th DGs[14] had a scrap and 'D' did some shooting. Retired to our old bivouac at 6 p.m. off-saddled & fed. had a feed at a cafe & marched again at 7.15 p.m. for Quievrain (20 mls). (3 Uhlans wounded brought in, in the morning by 4 DGs.) Marched all night without a halt partly thro' a bleak forest[15] where one of M's[16] guns turned over.

Sunday 23 August 1914[17]

Reached Quievrain at 3.30 a.m. after very tiring march. Went into billets, staff arrangements bad — all our horses in a narrow shed 250 yds long in a large string factory had to water passing buckets from a single pump. bedded down at 5.30 a.m. on the go for 26½ hours. Got up at 9 a.m. went out into a field to bivouac & waited for orders.[18] Marched out at 8.30 p.m. with 'D' and 'E' & some cavalry. Got to Baisieux (only 3 mls) at 12.30 a.m. & lay down to wait for dawn. A French airship passed over during the march.

Monday 24 August 1914[19]

Moved on at 3.30 & came into action near Marliere at 6 a.m. Took on a few Germans and made them retire. Aeroplanes of ours & the enemies flew over continually. Retired South about 2 miles & after waiting a couple of hours orders came for the cav. to occupy the same ridge again as the enemy had not come on. We went with De Lisle's bde[20] & were brought across the open where a heavy infantry &

43

gunfire was opened from their left from a wood. We had to cross a narrow rly. bridge & wheel, sharp to the right down one field across a dyke with only one crossing into the next field behind a hedge. 3 batteries got onto us before we were over the rly & galloped into action right under very heavy shell fire, losing 2 waggons. After 50 mins we got out by galloping up the teams & getting away down the hedge. Ammun was replenished by hand from the hedge. We got off about 400 rounds did considerable execution amongst the infantry and enabled what was left of the cavalry to withdraw, the bde suffered very severely but we were most extraordinarily lucky, 30 casualties & very few horses. Marston[21] was shot thro' the nose, Sgt Woodsford in the side; we carried him out to an ambulance. Gr. Pitt (my servant) & John & Brad's servants were all outed by one shell. We retired to Villers Pol[22] about 15 miles with the remnants of the cavalry & got there at 7.30 p.m. everyone done to the world. Marston was handed over to the Red X & Mundy[23] joined in his place. I was up till 10.30 p.m. waiting for orders & lay down till 12 a.m. when we hooked in & started forth once more, no baggage came in, but we had an excellent dinner with some good people with whom Brad was billeted.

Thursday 25 August 1914
Marched at 12.45 & lay down in a corn field five mls out till dawn, saddled up at 3.30 a.m. & spent all the morning falling back and coming into action once or twice, but no firing. The 18th Huss. maxim brought down a German aeroplane which was having a duel with one of ours or a Frenchman. In the evening we got hung up in a sunken road and just got off in time to prevent a disaster. I was at the tail of the column which was blocked in front by infantry transport which caused the greatest confusion, we got away at dusk with German Infantry getting very close in our rear,

having driven out our Infantry, causing terrible loss to the latter, especially to the South Lancs,[24] the wounded were bayonetted to death in many instances — we marched away expecting to make Ligny but after many orders & counter-orders we eventually lay down in a field with what cavalry they could collect, at 3.15 a.m. and got up at 4 a.m. & moved off at once.

Wednesday 26 August 1914
Parked in a field with the remains of the 1st and 2nd Cav Bgdes. & moved off at 7 a.m. with the intention of holding the German advance as far as possible & falling back gradually between Smith-Dorrien's army & Douglas Haig's[25] — came into action at 9 a.m. John's[26] section subsequently going forward to a nearer position at 1.45. Mundy took his section off with Major Mullins[27] just to our right. We hadn't shot yet. We saw an English battery wiped out by lyddite during the morning. Early in the afternoon[28] we all opened at cav. infantry & guns for some time, when the Germans opened on our ridge with big high explosive shell with the object probably of clearing the village just behind us. Sclater went out & brought John's section in & retired & Mundy retired at the same time, as soon as they went off I limbered up and followed — the shells were coming fairly thick, when we got to the edge of the village we heard a gun had been left there, so I sent the section on & took one of my limbers in with Bradbury. We found it was only a limber with a broken waggon body but as we were there we hooked it up & tied in the body with drag ropes & traces & brought it back, but the btty had gone on & left none to guide us, so eventually we picked up with the XIth H & retired slowly with them, then we struck the Clm & found the btty on in front of it. at 8 p.m. we started on a 10 ml march to bivouac, it was raining steadily by this time & very dark, I was at the rear of the Column with a troop of the IXth L. as

rear guard, we presently got the order 'files about from the front' & after returning some way I discovered it was only 2 squad's from in front of me coming back to hold the rear-guard who was being worried, so only having a wounded waggon I turned back again & groped after the Clm, which I eventually bumped into.

We got down to bivouac at 3 a.m. & got up again at 10 m to 4. Sclater & Bradbury were both very cooked & we were all sleeping on our horses, the men absolutely done up. Too weary to bother about dinner & lay down as I was on some straw. Got a glass of wine and bit of bread at 6 a.m.

Thursday 27 August 1914

We moved at 4.30 a.m. a few miles & trekked slowly to St Quentin (20 miles) passing on the way the scattered remains of 34th Bde RFA amm clm, the road was strewn for about 5 miles with howitzer & gun ammun. small arms ammun. and every description of stores, harness etc all abandoned, the Infantry were retiring in a pitiable condition done to the world the 5th Division.[29] We picked up any stragglers we could on our waggons & covered the retirement with the Cavalry. St Quentin was very congested with every description of troops & transport. We parked in a street with a fine avenue all down it, off saddled got ration & supplies & had a good meal with some kind French people. We moved out at 12 p.m. to get clear of the bridge over the river & formed up S. of the town to cover the retreat of the infantry at 5.30 p.m. We moved onto Seraucourt and billeted for the night in a large farm, full of prize cattle, spendid range of buildings & a large circular drinking trough in the yard. We slept in the house, a very big one, & messed on our own stuff & partly the owners who did all they could for us. & produced some priceless wine which we much appreciated. Got to bed at 12 a.m. & rose at 4 a.m. I slept on a mattress on a landing.

Friday 28 August 1914

Moved on a few mls — back towards St Quentin & formed up with patrols pushed out to and through St Quentin. Off saddled & cooked bacon in our mess tins. Continued the retirement at 11 p.m. (*sic*) & halted from 2.00–5 p.m., very hot, marched on another 8 mls & billeted at Berlancourt, the btty in an orchard & we in a farmhouse from which the inhabitants had fled. We made ourselves fairly comfortable on mattresses & got to bed at about 11.20 p.m. Heard that our baggage which we had not seen since our first fight, was 30 mls away!

Saturday 29 August 1914

Ready to move at 4 a.m. & stood by till 11 a.m. when we were suddenly attacked by a German force of Uhlans, infantry & field guns – we had most of the 1st & 2nd Cavalry Brigade with us. My section was ordered up to the N. of the village, & the rest of the btty retired the other side. It was very difficult country to see in & it was rather blind shooting but I did a bit of good, the cavalry got hotted a bit & we had a few shell round about but were not located. Retired after an hour and a half & fell back slowly to a position S of the village, Sclater taking 4 guns on the right & sending me with my two guns to watch the left. We did a good deal of shooting & I enjoyed several hours up in an apple tree,[30] eating delicious apples and shelling Germans! I had a bit of open country to watch & Uhlans & Infantry kept on coming down in extended lines but turned back every time when I got into them, range 2800' to 3200'. We fell back at about 3 or 4 p.m. The enemy's guns searched for us but never located us. We went back up the main Noyon Road to a position 2 miles away which was held by Infantry 2 bdes of IIIrd Division & a bdg of RFA Metcalf's battery being entrenched too. We sat down behind the slope & solemnly filled up with rations & supplies. I was sent back again with my section to the last position but having just got into action, a staff officer from S. Dorrien arrived & de Lisle decided to go back to him for orders & told us to fall back again. The Germans had retired & evacuated the village which was found empty by patrols of the 4th DGs who were now forward on the ridge we had been shelling, a report then came in that 2 squadrons of Uhlans were just entering the village again, so the cavalry left scouts back to watch & we retired, rifle bullets were pinging about before we left, as we topped the next rise we were shelled pretty heavily by the field guns & came into action again to cover the retirement. Nothing further happened & we marched back 10 miles through Noyon where we saw a spendid areoplane duel, the result of which was lost in the growing darkness. We got in billets at 10 p.m. at Baillie,[31] a field and deserted farmhouse, where we found enough mattresses etc. Motor transport was going thro' all the evening with ammunition. The cavalry lost a good many horses & a few men and the 4th DGs an officer Saunderson.[32]

Sunday 30 August 1914

A Europe morning at last! Breakfast at 8.30, move off 9.30. Had to shoot Marston's cob. We retired in peace to the cavalry divisional concentration in rear of the English army with a view to freshening up men & horses, badly needed after 10 solid days of rear guard fighting against very superior odds, never allowed to advance but just act as a bait to draw the Germans on. We marched slowly to Choisy au Bac & went into billets with most of the Cav Division all round. We had a perfectly charming house on the R. Aisne belonging to a Mme Binder Mistra[33] beautifully furnished, lovely old tapestry etc., comfortable beds, big bath & everything we could want, a very pretty garden running down to the river with a boat to get across to the lines in. There was only a caretaker who said that Madame had fled to Paris that morning with what she could stuff into 3 cars, she was very pleased to see us & produced wine of all sorts, & the gardener brought up a couple of rabbits & any amount of apples, melons etc. we could have done a rest cure there quite nicely. The bath was grand but rather spoilt by having to get into one's mushy clothes again. We found that the force we had been up against yesterday were mostly transported about in large motors, & some of them got into the woods round about & sniped a bit. Filled up with rations & supplies but our baggage waggon still absent.

Monday 31 August 1914

Moved at 4.30 a.m. via Compiègne a little way along the Amiens Road we had the whole cav division concentrated to cover the move west of the English army. IIIrd Bde took up a line to the N. & NW. We remained till 11.0 when we moved on. The bridge over R. Oise at Compiègne blown up behind us. A few Germans appeared & we took up a position along the Route d'Amiens, but nothing came of it & after being messed about backwards and forwards for most of the day we marched to Néry to bivouac, another 16 miles on. We had a room in a cottage & excellent straw beds on the floor of a sugar factory.

The 1st Cav Bde[34] were all in the village too.

Tuesday 1 September 1914

Got up at 4.0 a.m. with orders to be ready by 5 a.m. to move at a ¼ hrs notice, we had the teams all hooked to their carriages, poles down & everyone dismounted on our bivouac. I was trotting a horse down the road for lameness & was examining his hind fetlock, when suddenly a terrific burst of shrapnel & rifle & machine gun fire was opened onto us at a range of *600' to 800'*. No one had the slightest idea of there being any Germans in the vicinity, and I am not sure whether it was the fault of our own Cavalry or the French outposts.

The horse was killed at the first burst and I & Sgt Weedon dropped into the road and crawled along to one

The house at Baron in 1996 (see Jack Giffard's diary, September 1914.)

side of the camp & got up close to it under cover of some stacks. We found Bradbury, John Campbell & Mundy & about a dozen men there or so, we rushed out & got 2 guns into action, myself on one with ½ doz men & Brad, John & Mundy & the Sgt Major & Sergeant Nelson on the other.[35] I had only fired a few rounds when the whole of my crew were wiped out, so I went on till I'd finished the ammunition & then got hit through the left leg above the knee by a splinter & peppered on the right arm & back & grazed along the hip bone by a whole shell or a very large fragment. Then a shell pitched on the gun wheel & smashed it, something getting me on the top of my head, as I could do no good there, I crawled back to the stack where some of our wounded were sheltering, they were terribly knocked about most of them.[36] A few minutes later a shrapnel swept along our side of the stack, a fragment going clean through my right leg just above the knee in the inside & out underneath near the top of the leg, missing the main artery by an eighth of an inch, & I think missing the bone. 2 or 3 more pieces pierced the leg as well, several fellows were killed by it & horribly wounded. There was nothing for it then but to get the wounded as near under the stack as possible & trust to Providence. This terrific fire was kept up for sometime & eventually the Household Bde and 'I' Btty came up on the right & the Middlesex Regt on the left & we captured 10 guns and drove them off. The 1st Bde had done noble work especially with a machine gun de Crespigny[37] who was afterwards killed and the Germans never advanced a peg, the btty being knocked out. I think we did a good deal of damage & must have fired about 150 rounds. Mean while at the other guns they were behaving like heroes, & got knocked out one after the other. Poor Bradbury had both his legs taken off & died ½ hr later,[38] John was wounded & then killed outright & Mundy was badly hit in the legs, shoulders & head.

The sergeant major wasn't touched & Nelson only slightly wounded. Some of the stacks began to catch fire before the end, but thank God ours did not. Our casualties were of course enormous but I don't know for certain what. I know 2 teams were saved but believe not another horse escaped, poor Sealskin & Harriot were both killed, we did not lose the guns but that was practically all that remained of what 3 weeks ago left Aldershot the finest Horse Artillery Battery in the world.

I heard no definite news of Major Sclater Booth[39] but he was up at Headquarters at the other end of the village when the show started & I was told he had been sent down to the Base Hospital clean off his head.

The Cavalry suffered fairly heavily including poor Calley.[40] Briggs[41] was walking about as cool as a cucumber. About midday when the Germans had been driven off we were carried down on shutters to a house in the village &

Looking across the park to the village at Baron in 1996 (see Jack Giffard's diary, September 1914).

very roughly dressed, & about 5 p.m left with a big Field Ambulance Train. We wandered about & jolted for hours & eventually fetched up at Baron where a temporary dressing station had been fitted out in a large shooting lodge belonging to a French Baron.[42] There were 140 cases there, & 100 were sent on the same night in farm carts with straw beds to find their way to the base hospital outside Paris which is only 30 mls from here. The doctors dressed my wounds again & got me ready to go & gave me morphia for the journey but they either forgot me or filled up, as I was one of the left. The Field Ambulance hurried away again in the night & left 1 doctor & 20 men, nearly all reservists, as they knew the Germans would be in next day. My belongings consisted of 1 shirt, scarf, coat, handkerchief, 1 boot, 1 sock, ¼ of the left leg of my breeches & silk drawers.

Wednesday 2 September 1914

About 1 p.m a Prussian Uhlan patrol came in followed at 6 p.m by a regiment. Some effort was made either by English or French to turn them out with shrapnel & MG & rifle fire but to no purpose & Baron was soon full of Germans. They were very cheery & nice & told us it was all nonsense about the Russians advancing into Germany & that they had sunk a couple of English ships & not vice versa. They pinched everything they could lay hands on, food, watches, field glasses, maps, knives, scissors etc., & anything that took their fancy, also money. They went through all the kits & wards & even took the wristlet off a poor fellow who was delirious with a fractured skull. I just had time to hide all my things tied up in a handkerchief in the rafters.[43]

They left us very short of grub. I got a cup of tea by 10 p.m. & went to sleep with the morphia.

Thursday 3 September 1914

The Germans went carefully round the wards & took everyone who could walk & sent them off as prisoners of war & took ½ the staff too, leaving this place with 1 doctor & 13 men to look after 140 patients. Warrington[44] was the doctor & 10 of the men territorials or reservists. I am being looked after by a servant of Butler, 1st L Gds,[45] who was brought in last night shot through the lung. The town is full of Germans & sentries parade the wards at intervals. I had some of the splinters taken out of my arm & back. German Infantry came through at mid-day, & were very kind giving us cigarettes etc. Poor Mundy had his leg examined under chloroform and it was so terribly smashed he died about 8 p.m. 3 others died also.

Friday 4 September 1914

Did not sleep well, first night without morphia. Germans retiring all night thro' the town. A little musketry early in the morning. A good deal more metal extracted from my back but not all yet. At 5 p.m a very nice German officer came round, I think a Brigade Major, said he would do all he could for us & asked his brigade to send us some bread. He refused to let anything be touched by his men & ordered one to put back a pair of gaiters he had taken — shortly afterwards a General & his staff came round also extremely pleasant, but I fear the chances of our getting away, & even getting a letter to my poor old Babbles[46] is far away.

Saturday 5 September 1914

Henry's[47] birthday here's the best of luck to him. Slept better at regular intervals. Guard of 1 officer & 30 men were on all night. A pig was killed for us in the morning. Breakfast of 2 ration biscuits & tea. We have 5 cows to milk which have been left us so we are alright in that respect. Warrington re-dressed my wounds — & removed the field dressings which had been on for 3½ days, & put fresh gauze & bandages. They appear to be doing very well & I am gradually getting a little feeling into my right leg which has been quite numb ever since it was hit. We are getting very short of dressings etc & I don't expect to be touched again here, there are plenty of others who want it more than I. I am leaving the back altogether & let the rest of the splinters work out. No news yet & no sound of battle. It is weary work waiting & wondering what can be happening. A clean sheet over the mattress this morning but I must put up with the bloody coverlet.

The Germans brought a large mechanical musical box to amuse the patients, it played selections from the *Dollar Princess* & some other unrecognisable fragments. The Porker was excellent & tender & we had potatoes & some sort of marrow with him. A little gun fire began to the east at 2 p.m. Is Joffre at last beginning to cork up the neck of his much talked of bottle?[48] This continued till 5 p.m when rifle fire opened at the west of the village, supposed to be a French Patrol. Gunfire increased to NE & E & S. Renton is the name of the KDG's officer; he was with the Bays & got shot thro' the foot at the sugar factory.[49]

Sunday 6 September 1914

A perfect day after the last few cloudy & close ones. Gunfire & a little musketry opened about 7 a.m. but it's quite impossible to realise what is happening. The German officers a Uhlan & infantryman say they are round Paris & have only 40 men left here. They complain that they came out to fight the French & so far have seen nothing but English.

A good find of Pommery made this morning (called 'sec') but most likely 1914 & sweet! I looked at myself in a glass this morning, good Heavens! I am glad my friends can't see me. I hadn't realised that my last shave was just before that fatal day. I borrowed a heavy mowing machine of sorts from one of the Medical Sergts, and with some pain lopped off my beard — with the exception of a little clump on a splinter wound at the corner of my right jaw.

Had a good wash where possible also my teeth which up till now had to be done with a sharpened match. Hopkins (a 1st class fellow) found me a toothbrush somewhere in the house with plenty of wear in it yet, & a bottle of sweet dentifrice was divided out amongst us. Chocolate discovered now & tinned fruit, which provided a slap-up Sunday lunch with roast porker & white wine. Firing ceased altogether. Germans made our red X flag more conspicuous. About 5 p.m an English Cavalry patrol of 5 crossed the end of the park from N-S & were fired on. The hospital guard have entrenched themselves just under my window.

Had just settled down to go to sleep 8 p.m when an orderly rushes in to say the Germans wish to surrender as the place is surrounded by French who very soon arrive, disarm & take over the Germans & take possession. They have come from S. of Paris today & say that there are no Germans near Paris, they were originally up in Belgium & trekked back and move on N or E tomorrow.

Monday 7 September 1914

Heavy firing to S & SE started at 8 a.m. We got bread from French. Firing gradually to E and NE & ceased by 1 p.m. Had 2 hrs dressing of my wounds, & produced some more splinters, a big one from my hip. Had a wash with Asepso from tip to toe & put on a clean chemise! (?) of Mdm la Baronne, moved into Butler's room onto a mattress on the floor — 5 German Cavalry men passed thro' in the morning. An Inniskillen fusilier came in — said he escaped from the Germans 3 days ago.

At 3 p.m we sent out Hopkins & Trayes to go to Nanteuil Stn to find out if anything was doing there; 5½ miles out they met a German cyclists' patrol & 2 German MOs who chased them back here, but we hid them & they got no satisfaction & appeared to have no time to stop! About 6 p.m. three Uhlans & 2 cyclists passed thro'. The gun fire is slight & much further NE. Had to slit Madame's chemise into tails! can't stand a cylinder. A German Dragoon demanded an officer's cloak which he did *not* get. We made a picquet pack of a note book. 2 French soldiers came in, one of whom the German patrol shot with revolvers, dirty dogs.

Tuesday 8 September 1914

Got up into an armchair by the window with my right leg up — very weak and groggy. Two motors of French officers passed through. Small German patrol still hanging about.

Heavy firing to NE from 6 a.m. onwards, about 12 mls. Sent Hopkins to find out some means of our getting to Paris. Butler & I propose to go early tomorrow morning.

Hopkins just produced an aged native who can fit us out with a 4 wheel cart 4 horses and a cover, & man to show the way.

Russell produced a very very greasy pack of cards advertising Singer's machines which replaced the home made ones. Had a visit from a French lady & gentleman who said the French had gained a big victory at Meaux.[50] Right leg had to be dressed, still bleeding, really ought to be stitched but they cant do it here. Finally fixed up a bus & pair of horses with mattress on the floor, ready to start for Paris at 5 a.m. tomorrow. Gun fire started again at 6 p.m. it had died down about 2 or 3 p.m.

1 ofr)	Marched off	3 ofrs)	Died from	3 ofrs)	
				58 men)	
31 men)	prisoners	14 men)	wounds	1 of 14	left
				RAMC)	

Wednesday 9 September 1914

Called at 4 p.m. [sic] had a good breakfast of hot coffee & bread & jam. Put on a shirt & coat & carried down to the bus in which was a splendid bed of straw with a mattress on top. Butler Renton and Hopkins sitting on the seats.

The Jehu needless to say was late, but we sallied forth in great style at 6 a.m. flying the Red X flag. We passed a lot of French Troops & Transports *en route* & reached Le Plessis at 7.30 a.m. where we called at the Rly station & found there an ambulance train was leaving for Le Borget [sic], just outside Paris at 9 a.m., so we waited there, & French motors poured in with wounded meanwhile. Was transferred into a 1st class carriage with my mattress on the floor, French stretchers are smaller than ours but good enough. Eventually arrived at Le Borget at 11.30 where we were told no one was allowed to get out or enter Paris, & that we must go on to Rouen & get another train there for Havre where our base is.

French Red X Ladies invaded the train with coffee — grapes etc, at every station. We made a long halt at Mantes at 4 p.m. — where all the wounded were given bread, sardines, coffee, milk, tea etc — We were told that this train was for Rennes, Brittany — & not Rouen, but when all arrangements had been made to get out, & I was just being got into the stretcher, they decided we were going to Rouen. We got to within 10 miles of Rouen where we made a halt from 8–10 & all those who could walk got out & fed in a large hall place. We were brought dinner, excellent hot soup 2 fried eggs & some light cake & wine. At 1-oclock we reached Rouen & they started unloading the wounded into electric trams to run up to the big French base hospital. We wanted to stay on the station to be handy for the Havre train in morning.

Thursday 10 September 1914

But it wasn't until I had been placed thro' a tram window on a stretcher that we had our way, then they took us to an infirmary — in the refreshment rooms on the platform, about 20 beds run by the French *Croix-Rouge*, a most delightful lot of old ladies who could not do enough for us & talked & chattered away, it was no use thinking of sleep — It was 3 a.m. by now and our train went at 5 — so we had coffee at 4.30 & got ready when they decided there wasn't a train till 9.30. So we waited in patience, had another breakfast at 8.0 & a shave by the local barber & hoped to reach Havre by 1-0. It was an ordinary passenger train with a reserved carriage. My wounds had been bleeding a lot from the jolting & twisting about to see things on the way up, so the Matron swathed me all up again & I feel like a mummy. At one station we had a long chat with a lad from a racing establishment who could speak English pretty well, you can spot them in a minute even in France! After a good journey we reached Havre at 1.15 p.m. People loaded us with fruit, chocs etc., all the way up. Here we were told that all the English had moved out a week ago and there were only French Hospitals, so we telephoned through to one to send down an ambulance waggon & take us in. I had rather a rough handling in & out of the train as it was a narrow corridor. While waiting for the cart we got hold of the good lady who ran the refreshment room & she produced a table, & cooked us a delicious omelette, chocolate & cafe & rolls & butter. We drove up in an ordinary Military ambulance about 2 miles, thro' Havre to Frascati's Hotel,[51] which has been converted into a Hospital, an enormous building, on the edge of the sea, & my window looks right out onto the end of a pier with a lighthouse on it & the open sea beyond, & I can see the sunset. The sea washes right under the window. We had an excellent dinner about 6.0 & everything was most comfortable.

Friday 11 September 1914

Slept well till 4 a.m. breakfast 8.0, 2 eggs, chocolate & rolls. Had my wounds dressed at 10.0 by the senior surgeon, a very nice old man assisted by a gentleman whom I at once christened Mephistopheles, an assistant doctor, he fairly gloated over the wounds & tore the bandages off!! They were doing very well but had been knocked about a bit by the journey. Lunch at 11 or 12. Butler went to buy various necessaries in a taxi (nighties, hankies etc). Visited by Mrs Longstaffe & her daughter, her husband is the English shipping agents, also the Eng chaplain.

The Longstaffes brought some lovely roses, carnations, & sweet peas. They can get letters over by the Eng boat every night. The Chaplain brought a yesterday's *Daily Telegraph* which reported me as wounded. Later the Bishop of Belgium came to see us with his staff. A delightful fellow, not old, with beautiful red & gold hat & soft scarlet leather gloves. He was on his way to Antwerp via London.

It was dull & stormy all day & rained a lot.

Saturday 12 September 1914

The storm has broken leaving a very pretty sea, deep green & covered with white horses. My wounds were left alone. wrote letters most of the day. Miss Longstaffe and her brother paid me a visit & Butler went off to tea with them. The British Consul came, brought some Eng. papers & the latest official news, & said he had instructions from the Gov^nt to send over to England any wounded who wandered in. A lady also called who was nursing at another French hospital & she brought a lot of back *Daily Mirror*s. Turned wet in the evening & stormy. Mark Sykes[52] came up in the evening he crosses over tonight. Butler & Renton & the redoubtable Hopkins cross to Southampton by the 11-ock boat.

Sunday 13 September 1914

Very stormy sea but much clearer & glass rising. They must have had a bad crossing last night, had my wounds dressed by the Commandant, who brought another doctor in uniform with him who I hadn't seen before. Had visits from Mr and Mrs Longstaffe — Mayor of Havre, & President of the French *Croix-Rouge*. A lot of sweet peas from the boy scouts. A lot of French & a few German wounded came in with all sorts of trophies. such as Uhlan helmets. I get shaved every morning by a wounded French Infantry soldier — he was shot thro' the leg & is nearly well.

Monday 14 September 1914

Wet & stormy. Visit from a wounded French officer & a young Englishman in cotton business here, he brought me a lot of magazines & I gave him Sat's *Times*. Found out afterwards his name is Foster from Exmouth.

The Commandant dressed my wounds at 3 p.m. He took out a piece of my drawers from the right leg — which must have been drawn in & worked right through! My hip had come up big too. At 4 p.m I was moved in the *Croix-Rouge* motor ambulance to Mr Longstaffe's house where I was installed in a most comfortable room & enjoyed a real cup of tea.

It is nice to get back to an English establishment again. Two capable young French doctors are billeted in the House and look after me admirably. M^ss Willette and Lafon, the former son of the famous Parisian caricaturists — amusing & a very good sort.

Tuesday 15 September 1914

Slept well — severe nose-bleeding in the middle of the night. Quite a warm morning — what luxury an early morning cup of tea & marmalade for breakfast. Shaved by a villainous old man who keeps an ironmonger's shop & calls himself a barber. Went painfully over my face about six times with a very blunt razor & seemed rather to plant stubble into my beard then take it out! Never again! Peaceful day.

Wednesday 16 September 1914

Slept a little better with veronal sleeping draught. Dr Willette dressed my wounds after breakfast & spent about an hour at them, the right leg had a lot of pus at each end of the wound which is about 6 inches thro' & he got to work with the probe dipped in iodine very gently until at last he touched the nerve that is giving all the trouble. *Mon Dieu*! The other leg & hip are doing well. Willette is obviously 1st class & scrupulously clean. I was lifted onto a hammock chair whilst my bed was made & sat by the window.

Willette says it is imposible to say how long the nerve will be. Wired to Babbles & WO that I was crossing Thursday night & made all arrangements. At 3 p.m in walked Dad[53] and Muriel![54] & a trained nurse to take me over tonight so everything was fixed. I went down to the boat the *Lydia* at 5.30 in the Longstaffe's car — had a decked cabin with the nurse & we sailed at 10 p.m. Had a very good night, rough enough. The nurse being sick as a cat the whole way over. Babbles had sent every conceivable sort of thing I could possibly have wanted.

Thursday 17 September 1914

Arrived at S'hampton at 8 a.m. had to be examined by the Naval authorities off Isle of Wight. Taken to the train on a stretcher and reached Waterloo 11 a.m. met by Babbles, Mrs Long and Lady Scobell.[55] Taken to a Daimler private motor ambulance to Princess Henry of Battenburg's Hospital.

3

Eddie's Diary: The First Notebook

Thursday 4 November 1915

3 p.m. Left Waterloo for Southampton. D, P, M, M, J & M to see me off.[1] Stayed night at Railway Hotel.

5 November 1915

Found I did not sail till midnight, so nipped down to Weymouth to see Cicely:[2] got back 10 p.m., went on board *Hantonia*, which left 6 a.m. 6/11/15 for Havre:

6 November 1915

Delayed 4 hours at Spithead, arrived Havre 5.30 p.m., & reported, & went up to No.2 general base, camp 13.

7 November 1915

Got up after first night in sleeping bag: bit stiff from lying on floor. Nothing doing: so took a walk round. Warned at 1 p.m. to hold self in readiness to take draft.

5.30 started with draft marching to 'Gare Maritime', entrained for Rouen, draft showing bad discipline: like a mob of sheep.[3]

8 November 1915

Reached Rouen early morning: remained there all day, & orders to get ready to entrain at 4.45 p.m. (destination unknown). Left 5.35, another night in the train.

9 November 1915

Left Abbeville for Ailly-sur-Somme, which we reached at 9.30 a.m. Handed over draft, & left again for Abbeville at 12.45: stayed afternoon there, & left by 10.15 p.m. train: an hour late, & very uncomfortable carriage: & dirty.

10 November 1915

After 14 hours in train reached Harfleur about 2 p.m: Hungry! Heard at base camp that I was posted to 'Guards Division',[4] & leaving shortly.

11 November 1915

Still pouring with rain, & put on censoring letters all the morning, went down to Havre after lunch, to buy few things, & had tea with Swinford.[5] 8.30 p.m. reported at Camp Adjutant's office, & went down in motor lorry to la Gare Maritime at Havre: left 11.30 p.m. for Rouen.

12 November 1915

Turned out at Rouen about 7.20 a.m. spent the day there, & had a good bath and shave: wrote letters: left at 7.30 p.m., two hours late.

13 November 1915

Travelling all night at a slow rate: believe I am going to Bethune: very windy & cold. Reached B. at 12.45: stopped till 3 p.m., when I left for Merville my destination: at Lillers (3.57 p.m.) heard the first shots fired, from apparently quite close at hand. Went on past Merville to La Gorgue which I reached about 6 p.m. Found my way to

Hqrs of Artillery Guards Division. Two OMs[6] there, Capt Mann[7] and J. F. Ireland:[8] also Capt Trench.[9] Enjoyed a good dinner & very pleasant evening. Capt Trench kindly asked me to sleep in his room, where I enjoyed a good sleep in my 'Bag'.

14 November 1915
Met the general (Wardrope) at Breakfast: very nice man; & spoke very kindly of The Twins.[10] Went up (on horseback) to the 76th Bde Headqrs, with the General & Capt Trench, from there on to the Battery which I reached at 12 p.m. Spent rest of day looking round battery, which fired about ten rds. Met Captain Toppin[11] at 5 p.m.

2/Lieut E. H. Giffard October 1915.

15 November 1915
Went down with Capt & Dutton[12] to Ebenezer Farm; thence to OP,[13] where we registered (up to knees in water). From there went to another OP in Neuve Chapelle with Dutton, but failed to make communication with Battery. Got home at 5.30 p.m. Were quite near the German Trenches during the day & saw my first German shells bursting.

16 November 1915
Went down to the OP (Chateau) with D & saw the Test rounds fired. Then went to 'Winning-post', one or two shells burst near. Went to Company HdQtrs in 1st Line trenches

(3rd GGs) to fix up communication to Winning Post, thence to Battery: whilst here two German field HEs burst uncomfortably near overhead. Got home about 5.30 p.m.

17 November 1915
Left at 6.30 a.m. for Chateau OP: where I waited till the Capt came down, & saw the usual registering rounds fired: then waited for D^{14} at Scots Gds Hqrs & enjoyed a drink: got home to Battery at 1 o'clock: remained in rest of day. Headache evening.

18 November 1915
Remained with Battery all day; pay day: about 4.30 p.m. Capt got onto a German sniper's post with No. 2 gun & apparently demolished it: nasty wet afternoon. 28 HEs.

19 November 1918
Left at 6.20 a.m. for the OP at Chateau Redoubt, observed the registering rounds for X,^{15} reported at Ebenezer farm at 12 Noon, as Liaison officer. Went round front line trenches (Home Counties, Ducks Bill etc.) during afternoon: got back to Ebenezer farm at 4.10 p.m., & had dinner in the G Guards Mess. Good sleep.

20 November 1915
Went round front line trenches in morning & on to Chateau OP, which the General was inspecting: relieved of duty as Liaison officer at 12.15 p.m.; returned to Battery for lunch.
    No.3 gun fired 55 rds during afternoon.

Sunday 21 November 1915
Remained with battery, & visited advanced gun: received first mail here, since joining. Plum pudding for dinner.

22 November 1915

Left at 5.15 a.m. for OP (Chateau). Rather cold: registered for X: strengthened the place: discovered small cellar. Very foggy evening: got home at 5.30 p.m.

23 November 1915

Stayed with battery: 4th gun put in for next day's bombardment: started to rain in evening.

24 November 1915

Remained with battery, which fired 607 HE in 1¾ hrs & demolished barricade over signpost lane, & adjoining parapet for 40 yds or so. Relieved Semple[16] as Liaison officer in the evening.

25 November 1915

Went down to OP early & remained there all day: the CRA[17] looked in, in the morning: between 4 & 5 p.m. Germans began shelling heavily, so retaliated freely. Got back to Bn H-Qrs, & enjoyed cup of tea & buzzard cake:[18] also saw Winston C.[19]

26 November 1915

Went down to OP early, & returned to Ebenezer farm at 9.30 a.m., & was relieved by officer from C/76. Returned to Bty, half of which had moved off to new position near La Flinque. Snow fell: first I had seen for over 5 years.[20] Left with remaining half of battery at 6 p.m. Very cold evening: got guns in position, & ammunition deposited at 8.45: then enjoyed dinner, Mrs Rebbeck's[21] chocolate and cake.

27 November 1915

Sharp frost: looked round new billets, which are fairly good: laid out lines of fire for right section. Relieved S as Liaison officer left group: visited new OPs with Capt, & got shelled out of Dovecot: good thing as it is a most fragile structure. Returned to Scots Gds Bn H-Qrs; enjoyed a good evening with them.

28 November 1915

Got up at 6.30 a.m., & went to OP till 12 p.m.: relieved by Semple, & returned to battery: found parcels & letters: slept in dugout.

29 November 1915

Inspected new billets etc.: reported at road bend house at 12 p.m. to 3rd Grenadiers. Went down to OP in afternoon, & returned to Bn H-Qrs & enjoyed a good dinner etc.

30 November 1915

Got up at 6.30, had brekker, & spent morning at OP, retaliating etc. Returned to Battery for lunch & for rest of day: 'CDQ'[22] sent through in evening: 4 salvoes fired.

1 December 1915

Raining hard: found Gallagher (The Dr) was a Queenslander, & knew Sydney, NSW etc. well. Turned out a nice day: pipsqueaks[23] fell round our billets, & 4".2 in the afternoon on the right.

2 December 1915

4.2" over in the morning: went to OP in afternoon; & Road Bend House in the evening. Two salvos over battery in afternoon.

3 December 1915

Went down to OP in morning: very wet day: nothing much doing: returned to Battery in evening.

4 December 1915

Wet again: shelled by German light Howitzer during afternoon: no damage.

5 December 1915

Bombarded wire netting during afternoon: 549 rds. Germans retaliated on Battery first with Pipsqueaks & then with Howitzers: no damage. Went down to Bn H-Qrs in evening.

6 December 1915

Went down to OP in morning: very clear atmosphere during afternoon: Germans put two 5 inch into Billets: no casualties. We put 250 rds into netting.

7 December 1915

Relieved at OP by Dutton at 9 a.m.: returned to Battery. Billets evacuated: slept in Gunpit: disturbed night.

8 December 1915

Quiet day: *Estaminet* taken over by Battery, for reading room etc. Screen put up during evening. Reported at Road Bend House, 3rd Coldstreams (Col Campbell)[24] 5.30 p.m.

9 December 1915

Went down to OP in morning, & returned to battery in evening. Wet as usual.

10 December 1915

Went round billets etc., & reported to Bn H-Qrs in evening (Colonel McGregor).[25] *Estaminet* taken over by battery.

11 December 1915

Went to OP in morning; wet again, returned to Battery in evening: fired a good deal after dark.

Sunday 12 December 1915

Used the football before breakfast: men apparently enjoyed it: showery & very muddy: 4 pipsqueaks over battery: went to Bn H-Qrs in evening, 3rd Coldstreams. 4 weeks in the Battery!!

13 December 1915

Went to OP in morning: nothing much doing: Germans shelled Rue Tilleloy[26] during day. Returned to Bn H-Qrs in evening & thence to Battery.

14 December 1915

Minor operations: Left Group Batteries fired simultaneously at 11.35 a.m., on different houses. About 20 shells fell harmlessly around battery during afternoon: good for men so long as we have no casualties. Went to Bn H-Qrs 2nd Coldstreams in evening: got to bed at 3.30 a.m., & went to OP that morning:

15 December 1915

& remained at Bn H-Qrs another night. Atkinson[27] arrived at Battery.

16 December 1915

Went to OP in morning: very quiet day: raw & cold. Gen Cary[28] walked in during day. Returned to battery in evening.

17 December 1915

Spent day at battery preparing new position: very wet again.

18 December 1915

Foggy day: very quiet: working at new gun position.

Sunday 19 December 1915

Went to OP: twice evacuated it during German shelling.

Received overdue budget from Harfleur in evening: stomach bad in morning.

20 December 1915

Remained with Battery: wire-cutting during afternoon. Tobacco arrived.

21 December 1915

Wet again: went on with new Battery position: clothes for men arrived.[29]

22 December 1915

Went to OP: nothing doing during day: returned to Bty & went down to OP again at 8.30 p.m., to observe during expected gas attack (by us) but was put off at last moment.

23 December 1915

Rode down to La Gorgue in the morning; payday. Wet again: but still pretty mild.

24 December 1915

Showery again: a shell[30] in afternoon of ours unaccountably fell in our own trenches. Strafing during night & morning to annoy Germans.

25 December 1915

Christmas day. Went down to Village lounge: & found our men & Germans fraternizing[31] a little: but German shells on Rue Tilleloy put an end to it. Germans also asked for Armistice to carry away wounded from previous night's strafe: not granted. Enjoyed Erny's[32] cake for lunch: returned to Battery in evening.

Boxing day, Sunday 26 December 1915

Spent day at Battery: hamper arrived in evening; very good indeed.

27 December 1915

Went down to OP: very good light all day: OP shelled during afternoon. Returned to Battery: Turkey & plum pudding for dinner! Toppin returned, Cake by post.

The Rue Tilleloy, scene of abortive fraternization at Christmas 1915.

28 December 1915

Nice fine day: fired on by Huns twice during day: but gave more than we received. Toppin, Mess & papers moved over to New Billets. Gum boots came!!

29 December 1915

Went down to front line to observe the 'strafe' from 10 till 10.12 a.m.: nice sight. Returned battery: & slept in new billets (just outside Laventie) for the first time fairly comfortable.

30 December 1915

Went down to OP; nothing unusual to report. A mail from Collaroy[33] in the evening.

31 December 1915

Remained with Battery: fired on by huns in morning & afternoon, but no harm done. We strafed them with 100 rds in afternoon, 4 minutes. Heard in evening that my boots, the long lost, had turned up at home, so shall expect them soon!

1 January 1916

New Year's Day. Service & HC in *Estaminet*. Nothing much doing: a few pipsqueaks over in afternoon. Went down to Bn HdQrs, 1st Scots Guards, at Vangerie in evening: howling gale of wind.

Sunday 2 January 1916

Got down to OP at 6.30 a.m., in anticipation of our gas attack, which was again put off. Quiet day & wet: remained at Bn HdQrs another day.

3 January 1916

Went to OP in morning: very good light: returned to billets in evening. 2 officers of 38th Division joined for instruction & 28 men. Battery in new position near fort D'Esquin.[34]

4 January 1916

Remained with battery: steel hut gun pit put up. Germans were very active for a change.

5 January 1916

In Battery during the day: quiet day settling into new position: went down to Bn HdQrs in evening: 1st S Gds.

6 January 1916

Went to OP early: Huns shelled Bn HdQrs fairly heavily during day: tried to catch some Huns myself at N 26 C 8.3½. Returned to Battery in evening.

7 January 1916

In Battery during day: Huns sent about 50 4.2s between Battery and Fte D'Esquin. Slept in Bty.

The new Fort D'Esquin. See Eddie Giffard's Diary around Christmas and New Year 1915–16.

8 January 1916

Nice fine day. Stayed in Bty & Billets during day. Huns heavily shelled (with 5.9" at least!) & 4.2"'s, old Bty position & *Estaminet*. Lucky we were not there. Went to Bn HdQrs at Hougemont[35] House in evening; 3rd Grenadier Gds. Hair cut in afternoon.

Sunday 9 January 1916

Went to OP in morning: very quiet day: a few hun shells in the evening. Returned to billets. Toppin went away in evening to Oire.

10 January 1916

Went down to La Gorgue & waggon line: lunched at BAC (76th) Beysdon, Major G-Waterman, Sherridan & Scott-Deacon.[36] Got back at 4.30 p.m. Huns were putting coal boxes[37] over the Laventie road. Went down to Bn-Hd-qrs in evening, 1st Scots.

11 January 1916

Went to OP, fairly quiet: met Paul Methuen[38] in the trenches. Returned to Bty in evening.

12 January 1916

Remained with Bty, & slept there in evening. At dusk had minor operations, with usual object of killing Germans.

Rain during the night: & cold wind.

13 January 1916

Went down to OP at 10 a.m.; 4.2"s were falling round it. Splinter pierced my clothes & drew blood at top of right thigh: applied iodine as precaution: otherwise no harm done. Went to Hougomont in evening to 2nd Scots Guards.

14 January 1916

Went to OP in morning: Germans very active with artillery along Rue Tilleloy: nice day though cold. Returned to Billets in evening.

15 January 1916

Rode down to waggon line: spent the day there, lunching at BAC.

Sunday 16 January 1916

Cicely's[39] birthday. Went down to OP at midday, & to Bn HdQrs in evening (Welsh Guards): fine day.

17 January 1916

OP in morning: very quiet day: returned to Billets for lunch: slept Bty in evening.

18 January 1916

Warm day, & drizzling. Remained in Bty, & returned to Billets for tea.

19 January 1916

Rode down to waggon line in morning. Went to OP at 1 p.m.: thence to Bn HdQrs Welsh Guards: small artillery strafe in evening.

20 January 1916

Went to OP early, & returned to Billets 1.30 p.m.: thence to Bty 4.30 p.m., for night.

21 January 1916

Fine day: nothing much occurred during day: received parcel of socks, mittens etc., slept in billets.

22 January 1916

Rode down to waggon line in morning, & went to OP at one o'clock: good light in afternoon: flashes of German light How very visible. Went to Bn HdQrs Hougomont, 2nd SGs in evening.

Sunday 23 January 1916

Went down to OP early: foggy morning: returned to billets at 1.30. Germans did a lot of shelling during afternoon over Laventie etc. Went to Battery at 5 p.m.: & to Bn HdQrs to relieve D for 2 hours: Burston[40] joined the Battery.

24 January 1916

Remained in Battery during day: very busy, firing at

intervals during the day. Returned to billets in evening.

25 January 1916
Rode down to waggon line in morning: & went to OP at 1 p.m. CRA house heavily shelled. Bn HdQrs in evening.

26 January 1916
Went to OP in morning: & to Battery in evening: firing all night: not much sleep: took in 500 rds of ammunition at 3 a.m. 27/1/16.

27 January 1916
Heavy bombardment by us in the early morning. Otherwise fairly quiet during the day: went back to billets in evening.

28 January 1916
Rode down to Waggon Line in morning: went to Bn HdQrs in evening, 3rd G Guards.

29 January 1916
Went down to OP in morning: minor operations. Asked for address, & station! Sounds promising for leave!

Sunday 30 January 1916
Very foggy: remained in Bty: received notice at 4.30 p.m. to proceed on leave: 1.30 a.m. from La Gorgue. Reached 76th Bge 10 p.m. & went to train at 11.15.

31 January 1916
Reached Boulogne at 8.15 a.m.: had to waste most of the day there. Left at 4.30, for Folkestone 6.10 p.m. Left for Town at 7.35: had to stop for 1½ hours at Sevenoaks owing to zeppelin[41] (D--n him!). Reached Victoria about 11 p.m. Stayed night at Paddington Hotel.[42]

1 February 1916

Left for Marlborough by 7.30 a.m. train:[43] arrived there at 10 a.m.

Have to leave Victoria again on Thursday Feb 10th.

4

Eddie's Diary: The Second Notebook

This notebook is inscribed 'from Robina'.[1] It starts with a message addressed to Lieutenant Dutton, D/76 Battery, Guards Division. 'Delayed please send horse Friday night. Giffard.'

Return to Front after First Leave

Thursday 10 Feb 1916

Left Victoria 9.15 a.m.: seen off by D, P, May and Maud. Arrived Folkestone 11.5 a.m. lunched at Royal pav Hotel, and went aboard *Queen* at 1.30 p.m.: finally sailed at 3.20 p.m., reaching Boulogne at 5.15 p.m. Stayed at Hotel Meurice for night.

11 February 1916

Left B at 1.20 p.m., & arrived La Gorgue 7.15 p.m. Got lift up in C/76 Cook's cart: reached Billets 8 p.m. Found Battery had had to take up another position 200 yds in rear. OP all knocked out.

12 February 1916

Got up 5.30 a.m.: a good start in again. Went to Dovecot, & then to front line with Dutton, for wirecutting. Got back to Battery 5.45, & stayed there for the night.

Sunday 13 February 1916

Remained in battery all day: busy working on the 'new' position: went to billets in evening.

Definitely heard we go out for 9 days rest soon, & then to Ypres.

14 February 1916

Went to OP again: very windy & so quiet: Dovecot very shaky. Returned to billets.

15 February 1916

OP till one o'clock: very windy: Battery in evening.

16 February 1916

Gale of wind & rain: right section expected to be relieved but was not. Another night in battery.

17 February 1916

Went down to OP: waiting to be relieved by the Irish Division.

Relieved at 1.30 p.m.: then took left Section² down to Waggon line: & from there whole Bty went to camp at billets between La Gorgue & Merville.

18 February 1916

Remained the whole day: very wet & gale in evening.

19 February 1916

Got up at 3.45 a.m. left 6.30 for Arneke, which we reached at 3.30 p.m., passing through Hazebrouck. Rest billets at last: one gun got stuck in mud for an hour: but got in at 4.30 p.m. Dined at Hotel: & had some music with A/70.

Sunday 20 February 1916

Went out to exercise horses: nice sunny day. Orders to move 6 miles the next day to fresh billets.

21 February 1916

Left at 10 a.m. for Zeggers Cappel, which we reached at 12 p.m.: billeted in a farm house: nice Mess, but poor place for sleeping. Eringhem.

22 February 1916

Getting down to 'rest'. Cherry Brandy arrived!!

23 February 1916

Cold and snowing: Football match in afternoon in the snow.

24 February 1916

Very sharp frost, & slippery roads: nice fine day. Henry's[3] Christmas letter arrived. Burston went over to A/76: AEW[4] inspected Battery.

25 February 1916

Very hard frost: no sun, cold day & more snow in afternoon. Roads too slippery for exercise.

26 February 1916

Frost again: fair day: cold.

Sunday 27 February 1916

Church parade.

28 February 1916

Bty inspected by General Fielding, GOC[5] Division: concert at Zeggers Cappel.

29 February 1916

Very muddy: more rain in evening.

1 March 1916

Nice warm day, but very muddy: much work on horses preparing for show.

2 March 1916

Nice day: rode into Esquelbec: cake arrived in evening, also more rain.

3 March 1916

Dull, wet day: exercise etc. Ireland[6] and Batten-Poull[7] to dinner.

4 March 1916

Cold: rain & sleet.

Sunday 5 March 1916

Rain & sleet showers: cold.

6 March 1916

More snow on the ground: thaw later: map reading: rode to Colehill [?] in afternoon: decided on getting gramophone etc for Battery.

7 March 1916

Snowing & half thawing all day: very wet & muddy.

8 March 1916

2 inches of snow: nice sunny day: horse show at Zeggers-Cappel: quite a success.

9 March 1916

Hard frost: same work as usual.

10 March 1916

Cold raw day, with sleet showers: range-finding lesson. Ride in afternoon. Left section ordered to leave on 14th for new position: long march in prospect.

11 March 1916

Rode to Zeggers Cappel, & from there motor-bussed to Houtkerk via Esquelbecq, Wormhout, & Herzeele: & saw new waggon lines, which were very satisfactory, got home at 4 p.m.

Sunday 12 March 1916

Took Church parade to Zeggers Cappel: & met Pat McCormick,[8] who took the service: very nice sunny day.

13 March 1916

Nice sunny day. Got hair cut at Arnecke. P. McCormick came to Lunch. Preparations for moving the Left section on following day.

14 March 1916

Another sunny warm day. Left Billets with left section at 8 a.m.: arrived at Houtkerk with guns & detachments at 12.30 p.m.: guns and baggage left 2.30 p.m. Left in Motor Lorry at 5 p.m. for Ypres: through Watou (crossed into Belgium at 5.35 p.m.) Abeele & Poperinghe, & Vlamertinghe: arrived Ypres at same time as guns at 7.15 p.m.: quite nice quarters.

15 March 1916

Easy day: went down to OP in afternoon with Majs. Robertson & Toppin:[9] a good deal of shelling going on: first taste of the 'salient'. Came back past Cathedral & Cloth Hall: both in utter ruins.

16 March 1916

Went down to OP to 'find my way about', with Appleby of 42nd Bty.[10] Fair amount of shelling: good clear day.

17 March 1916

Went down in afternoon to Forward gun, & Bn HdQrs with R.[11]

18 March 1916

Slack day: many Hun aeroplanes about: warm day.

Sunday 19 March 1916

Went to OP early: & to Bn Hd-Qrs in evening: right section came in during day, without any accident.

20 March 1916

Returned to OP in morning: good deal of shelling by the Huns: Bty position also shelled.

21 March 1916

Foggy day, less shelling; but we get very careful now.

22 March 1916

Went down to frontline trench early: very badly protected, but are evidently getting better. Spent rest of day in Battery: wet day.

23 March 1916

Rode down to Poperinghe: & went to OP in the afternoon: parcel of socks arrived in evening.

24 March 1916

Remained in Battery: snow on ground in morning: T went home on 10 days leave.

25 March 1916

Remained in Battery: fairly quiet.

26 March 1916

Went down to OP at 6 a.m. and to Bn HdQrs Potize (2 SGs) in evening. Went back to Battery at 6.30 a.m.

27 March 1916

Cold wind: heavy firing down South.

28 March 1916

Heard of success at St Eloi.[12] Went to OP, which was shelled during morning: rather unpleasant: returned Bty in evening.

29 March 1916

Went down to OP early: cold morning & snowing: quiet day.

30 March 1916

Nice sunny day: Huns very active with aeroplanes in morning: & heavily strafed our 2nd line in afternoon: to which we replied fairly heavily. During night Germans continued to heavily 'strafe' our 1st & 2nd lines, & continued till 4 a.m. of 31st with intervals.

31 March 1916

Got out of bed at 3 a.m., & kept firing till 6 a.m., to form barrage: things then quietened. Lovely day, huns very active in the air: went to OP & Bn HdQrs in evening: 3rd Grenadiers.

1 April 1916

Went to OP. Very quiet day: Bty in evening.

Sunday 2 April 1916

Beautiful spring day: visited reserve position in afternoon. Big Strafe all night at St Eloi.

3 April 1916

Went down to OP: lovely day again: registered for the strafe of the next day!!

4 April 1916

Strafe duly commenced but owing to bad light was postponed at midday. Toppin returned in evening.

5 April 1916

Strafe took place: heavy guns taking part: apparently, a success: Germans did not retaliate much. Dutton went on leave in evening.

6 April 1916

Went to OP: quiet day: BHQ in evening, 1st Scots.

7 April 1916

Remained in battery for the day, very quiet.

8 April 1916

Went round to OPs in morning, & to OP in the evening to observe flashes.

Sunday 9 April 1916

Spent day in Battery: fairly quiet.

10 April 1916

Quiet day: but we were pulled out of bed at 3 a.m.: during our gas attack on the right (when craters at St Eloi were again retaken by us). Went down to OP and advanced gun in morning.

11 April 1916

OP early & Bn HdQrs: heavy bombardment by huns on left.

12 April 1916

Remained in Bty.

13 April 1916

Went to OP & BHQ in evening, 3rd Coldstreams.

14 April 1916

Returned to Bty in morning: very wet & windy day. Heard of new niece.[13]

15 April 1916

Went out early to Forward gun & OP etc: returned to breakfast. OP was pipsqueak[ed] during day.

Sunday 16 April 1916

Nice Spring day: went out for a walk round OPs etc. early with Major. Found Bob's grave[14] in cemetery. Visited by General Wardrope[15] after breakfast.

Service in the evening. Gramophone arrived & games etc from Comforts fund.

17 April 1916

Wet windy day again. Remained in Battery, Cake, books & chocs from Auntie.[16]

18 April 1916

Went to OP: very wet day. BHQ in evening, 2nd Coldstreams.

19 April 1916

Quiet during day: German attack in evening, on our left: supposed to have entered our trenches & been 'booted' out again.

20 April 1916

Left at 9.15 for waggon line, which I reached at 1 p.m.: found McQueenie [17] of C/76 staying in our 'chateau'. Quite a neat little place.

21 April 1916

Rode into Houtkerque, & met Burston.[18] Spent remainder of day in waggon line. Gen Evans[19] visited us: & Hindmarsh, his ADC was also there.

22 April 1916

Pouring wet day, & cold wind: horses must feel it very much.

23 April 1916

Easter Sunday. Nice sunny day. Service in evening by Hubbard.[20]

24 April 1916

Nice day again: early exercise. Dined at Bge HdQrs in evening: heard that I had to leave for firing line again next morning.

25 April 1916

Rode back to Bty calling at Bge HdQrs, & BAC on the way: reached battery at 4.30 p.m., & went on down to OP & Bn HQ, 2nd CG.

26 April 1916

Returned to Bty in morning. Heavy bombardment at St Eloi in evening & bombing attacks, by Germans.

27 April 1916

Beautiful weather still. Went down to OP & AG in morning: still expect to have leave any moment.

28 April 1916

Remained in Bty.

29 April 1916

Got up at 2 a.m. & went down to front line with the Major, returning for breakfast to Bty.

30 April 1916

Went down to OP early: remained all day, & to BHQ Welsh Gds in evening: heard of Kut's fall[21] — the d----d government.

1 May 1916

Beautiful day again: went to OP early, & returned to Bty to breakfast.

Huns shelled Water Tower the whole morning, most unsuccessfully. 'Orders' to proceed to GDA for leave warrant: dined at GDA, and slept at Talbot House,[22] leaving Poperinghe by 4.45 a.m. train.

2 May 1916

Reached Boulogne at 10.45, & Folkestone 1 p.m. London 3.35, & caught five o'clock from Paddington.

Second Return from Leave

13 May 1916

Left Victoria at 7.50 a.m.: seen off by the family. Had to remain all day at Folkestone: & left for Boulogne at 7.30 p.m. Remained there for the night at Hotel De Vaux.

14 May 1916

Remained all day at Boulogne to catch 7.15 p.m. train for Poperinghe: rather a waste of two days. Met the Major in the evening.

15 May 1916

Reached Poperinghe at 2 a.m., and slept at Talbot House: went up to Battery by Motor bus, & reached 'home' at 1 p.m. OC & sub of A/91 also came.

16 May 1916

Rode down to Poperinghe & went through the gas test, & visited waggon line. Gunter's cake[23] arrived in evening. Fine day.
   D/76 Bty changed to C/61.

17 May 1916

Remained in Bty: quiet day.

18 May 1916

Beautiful day again: good deal of Artillery activity: went down to C/74 in morning.

19 May 1916

Went to OP early and BHQ (3rd GGs) in evening.

20 May 1916

Went to OP at 4 a.m.: relieved in afternoon by A 91. Walked to Vlamertinghe & Motorbussed to La Cloche.

Sunday 21 May 1916

Nice hot day: nice billets on the whole, usual 'Rest' routine.

22 May 1916

Fine hot morning: wet evening: Country looking very different to last March.

23 May 1916

Reveille 5 p.m. [*sic*] every morning now.

26 May 1916

Rode to Wormhoudt for the Battery money: fairly busy all rest of the day.

27 May 1916

Fine day, went for usual exercise & grazing: very busy over equipments etc.

To 7 June 1916

Regular routine: stables, exercise, etc etc. News of Battle of Jutland came in:[24] also attacks by Huns round Ypres.

Just heard today of K's death,[25] & all his staff: Great blow to the Country!

11 June 1916

Rumours of our going back to Ypres shortly; cheerful news of Russian victory over the Austrians. Rumour of Kaiser's death also came in: can't say truthfully that I should be sorry.

12 June 1916

Went out to field day near Volckerinckhove: Infantry attacked imaginary German trenches: with a view to future operations!

13 June 1916

3rd day of heavy rain: horse lines in a fearful mess.

14 June 1916

Heard that I proceed with advance party to Ypres, on the next day.

15 June 1916

Motor-bussed up to Ypres from Zeggers-Cappel: taking over from 21st Battery (Major Boyd). Very quiet: daylight saving bill came into force.

16 June 1916

Nice weather again: visited OP in afternoon: difficult Zone.

18 June 1916

Battery detachments arrived early: went to OP at 1 p.m. till 9.30 p.m. OP consists of trench, & periscope.

23 June 1916

Nothing much happened since the last entry: settling in & finding one's way about, registering etc.

25 June 1916

Liaison Officer 1st G Gds. Went down to front line with Major Thorne[26] while they were digging new trenches: quite successful. Just popped the parapet!

29 June 1916

Fairly wet weather the last few days: all sorts of rumours of operations.

1 July 1916

Day of great offensive! Strafe on all day (by us), also at night: Infantry on our left retook Mortelaye [?] *Estaminet*, which had only 2 men in it.

7 July 1916

Nothing much happened here lately: news of our offensive in the South came through.[27] All hope it is the beginning of the end. A rumour that we are going South, & fairly likely too. Plans for taking of 'High Cmd Redoubt' all cancelled apparently. Southern offensive does not seem to have got on quite so well the last 2 days.

10 July 1916

Went down to Waggon line for a spell: Atkinson[28] going to

firing line: dinner at Skindles in the evening, with Webster[29] who came down for one night's bust.

18 July 1916

After pleasant week at Waggon Line returned to Battery on 18th. Took over Dutton's job on the Gun pits: out all night on it.

20 July 1916

Bedroom blown in by a 5.9": no damage to kit.

23 July 1916

Heard definitely that we are to be shortly relieved by the 4th Division. This looks like South for us.

26 July 1916

Heard from home that I had got my second star, dated May 1st.[30]

28 July 1916

Orders, move down to waggon line with 1 & 2 guns tonight: arrived Waggon Line at 3 a.m. on

29 July 1916

Left our lines at 12 midday: arrived at new waggon line (between Esquelbec & Arneke) at 7.45 p.m.: very hot & dusty march: dark by the time we were settled down.

30 July 1916

Remaining two guns arrived about 5.45 a.m. Remained all day in billets.

31 July 1916

Left at 10 a.m., for Cassel: entrained & left at 3.50 p.m. reaching St Previn at 7.40 p.m. & Camp at 2 a.m. on 1/8/16.

1 August 1916

Remained all day in billets 2 Ks from Doullens, & went out 'fishing' with the Major on the D'Authie.

2 August 1916

Marched at Midday to Thievres: 9 miles very hot & dusty. In & settled down at 4.30 p.m.

4 August 1916

Rode up with Marsh[31] (who joined previous day) to the new Bty position near Colincamps. C 119 RFA (38th Div). Very nice country like Salisbury Plain.

6 August 1916

Took left section up to new Battery position in evening; arriving 9.30 p.m.

7 August 1916

Remained in Battery: Marsh & right Section came up in evening.

8 August 1916

Went to OP early, & to BHQ, 12th Bn RB (observation wood) in evening.

14 August 1916

Nothing much happened during last few days: news good all round. We seem to be progressing rather slowly on the Somme. Today is the first proper wet day for a month about: showery.

15 August 1916

Went down to Waggon line in afternoon with Major to Authie-St Leger.

16 August 1916

We now have Guards Infantry in front of us: & expect that whole division is moving further south; (The right of our line?).

17 August 1916

OP all day & Bn HdQrs 2nd Coldstreams in evening.

20 August 1916

Gds Infantry go out: relieved by 2nd Div. We stay in.

24 August 1916

Biked down to Waggon line, lunching at 61st Brigade Hd-Qrs on the way. Rode home.

25 August 1916

Heard that we go out in two days time, being relieved by 2nd DA.

26 August 1916

Went to OP early & to BHQ in the evening: Essex Regiment.

27 August 1916

1 section of relieving Bty (71st of 2nd DA) came up & relieved A & D subs.[32]

28 August 1916

Remainder of Battery went down to Authie-St Leger for night: marched next morning at 7.30 a.m. 29/8/16 for Famechon, for billets. Very wet weather: tremendous thundershowers in afternoon: found dry billets for men.

30 August 1916

Wet day again: remained at Flamecon [*sic*].

31 August 1916

Fine day: marched at 1 p.m. for Rainneville, via Marieux & Puchevillers: stayed there the night.

1 September 1916

Left at 10.15 a.m. for Mericourt L'Abbe via Corbie. Arrived in Camp at 4.15 p.m. Not far from the 'big push'.

3 September 1916

Left Mericourt for Bois de Taille, which we reached at 3 p.m. Great news of advance past Guillemont & Ginchy. Right Section at 4.30 the next morning for the Guillemont Front.

4 September 1916

Pouring wet most of the day.

5 September 1916

Reveille 2.30 a.m.: Left for new waggon [line] at Meaulte at 5 a.m.: reached Bty position at 8.45 a.m.: between Longueval windmill & Trones Wood:[33] shelled during morning with 5.9" & 8", & 77 mm: Narrow trench came in useful: no damage.

6 September 1916

Remained in battery: 11 a.m. usual (apparently) morning strafe with 5.9" & 4.2": no damage to our own battery: but New Zealand 4.5" & entire pit blown up 40 yds on left. Working all day on trench, amm. dump etc.

7 September 1916

Went to Bornafay Wood to meet Colonel at 7.30 a.m., but failed! Remained in Battery during rest of the day: usual Bombardment.

8 September 1916

Battery in morning & went to see OP at arrowhead Copse. Ginchy to be attacked to-morrow: shall start for Bn HdQrs at 10 p.m. Arrived BHQ of Royal Munsters[34] at midnight: had a somewhat uncomfortable sleep in the telephone pit.

9 September 1916

Moved on about 500 yds, & remained in an old german dugout during the morning:

Intense bombardment began at 4.30: at 4.45 the 47th & 48th Bge popped the parapet. Ginchy was soon secured & Consolidating was soon begun. German artillery was very active during the day, especially round Guillemont. There was a good deal of mixing up of Battalions of 48th Bge. The Welsh Gds & 4th G Gds came up at midnight & relieved the tired 16th Division: Germans shelled fairly heavily the area between Ginchy & Guillemont: remained during night at Bn HdQrs in Ginchy of 1st Munsters.

10 September 1916

Position on our right still obscure, for Welsh Gds had not got in contact with Grenadiers on their right. Went down to HdQrs of Welsh Gds at Guillemont at 7 a.m. to see the OC, & with message from Col Mount Mason of the Munsters: relieved by Minton, & returned home to Battery which I reached at 9.30 a.m.: operations of preceding day appear to have been very successful on the whole: a good few prisoners being secured.

Enjoyed a good rest.

11 September 1916

Went with the Major early to Guillemont, & returned to Battery for breakfast: remained in Battery: Big strafe near Delville Wood[35] in the early part of night: Huns apparently had wind up.

12 September 1916

We appear to be progressing well: our Heavies very active all morning: we appear to have a Colossal amount of Artillery.

13 and 14 September 1916

Preparatory bombardment for the great attack: Cavalry all massed behind: first appearance of 'Tanks'.[36]

15 September 1916

Intense bombardment began at 6.20 a.m.: assault at 6.32: various rumours about our progress during the morning.

We have apparently done fairly well: Battery moved forward to East of Trones Wood in the evening. Settled down to 3 hrs sleep at 3 a.m. on 16/9/16.

16 September 1916

Rather reluctantly went down to the waggon line for a few days change, Webster relieving me: have had a heavy cold the last 3 days.

Sunday 17 September 1916

Very wet, & Lines in a shocking state: horses falling away rather badly.

18 September 1916

Very wet: drove over in Cooks' cart to Mericourt to buy stuff for the Mess.

19 September 1916

Very heavy going: took 6 waggons up to move amm. from old to new position. Met Dutton on way back & had tea with him.

20 September 1916

Appears to be a very heavy bombardment in direction of Combles or Peronne.

21 September 1916

Weather clearing a bit.

22 September 1916

Went back to firing line, relieving Atkinson.

23 September 1916

A few 4" gun shells over Bty in morning: 4 horses knocked out: weather improving considerably.

Sunday 24 September 1916

Went up with Major to signallers dugout early: heavy fog: eve of another 'attack', much artillery preparation.

25 September 1916

Furious bombardment previous to attack, which took place at 12.45 p.m. Guards apparently fulfilled their task perfectly: the Division working like a machine: Group & Bge congratulated by the Corps Commander[37] on 'brilliant achievement'. Went to find new battery position with Major in evening: 'Forward' to-morrow.

26 September 1916

Got up at 1.30 a.m., & left with two waggons of material at 3.30 for new Battery position between Ginchy and Les Boeufs:[38] some difficulty in finding the way. Worked hard up till 3 p.m., when I heard that we had to go further forward: all labour in vain.

Later. After all we moved into the prepared position about midnight.

27 September 1916

Bty spent the day 'consolidating': went to OP, & had my first view over Bapaume etc.

28 September 1916

Remained in Bty, finishing off dugouts etc.

29 September 1916

Went up at 6.30 a.m.to relieve Foley[39] at OP: very foggy: no view: dull day.

30 September 1916

Returned home from OP at 7 a.m.: cold & fine.

1 October 1916

At 1 a.m. we came back to normal time. Battery was shelled a fair amount by 4.2" between 2 & 3 p.m.: no damage done: & fairly lucky: small advance in front of Les Boeufs apparently quite successful.

2 October 1916

Very typical Autumn day foggy in morning, & rain in evening: everything very mucky, & roads terrible.

3 October 1916

Ditto.

4 October 1916

Rain again: went to OP with Major: cleared up a bit in evening.

5 October 1916

Shells fell at intervals round Battery practically all day: one or two lucky escapes: Bombardier Huttlestone buried in his dugout, & taken to Dressing station with bad shell shock & bruises.

6 October 1916

Fine day: walked down to waggon line at Carnoy: enjoyed good lunch & hot bath. Rode back part of the way in evening.

7 October 1916

Went to OP, & watched attack in afternoon, when we took the 'Brown' line[40] preparatory to Le Transloy: heavy Hun barrage most of the evening.

8 October 1916

Wet again & very mucky: remained in Battery.

9 October 1916

Remained about Battery.

10 October 1916

Went early to BHQ, & tried to lay a wire: went round trenches, held by 6th Div.[41] Heavy German fire most of the day from front line to sunken road between Gueudecourt & Les Boeufs.

5

Eddie's Diary: The Third Notebook

11 October 1916

Went round front trenches early with Bn CO: & met Colonel Buzzard[1] on way back & stopped with him during the morning: got home to Bty (breakfastless) at 2 p.m. Heard Gunner Murphy had been killed & Gunner Dalton wounded.

12 October 1916

Remained in Battery: attack on brown line continued in afternoon: a little ground gained, but on the whole rather a failure: Very heavy Enemy fire, when attack commenced: evidently they were well prepared for it.

13 October 1916

In Battery: mild cloudy weather: 5.2" gun was rather objectionable during the night.

14 October 1916

Remained in Battery.

Sunday 15 October 1916

Attack at 5.30 a.m.: fairly successful: went down to BHQ

where remained all day & night: wires broken several times: rather a hot spot.

16 October 1916

Fresh sunny day: returned from BHQ to Bty.

17 October 1916

Went to OP.

18 October 1916

Remained in Battery.

19 October 1916

Went down to Bn HdQrs: very wet day: & trenches appalling: dried myself a bit in dugout during the night: the Infantry must have had a rotten time.

20 October 1916

Returned to Battery: turned quite cold, with a nip of frost.

21 October 1916

Still very cold: Major went to Waggon Line for bath, & I remained in Bty: as before Bty was shelled a good deal: Bombardier Clarke J was wounded, & his horse had to be shot.

22 October 1916

Walked down to waggon line & back: had tea with Dr (Harris) on way back.

23 October 1916

Remained in battery: big attack in afternoon, which fairly successful.

24 October 1916

Disturbed by Major at 1 a.m.: firing from then on to 4 a.m. during attack on Zenith trench: Wet day again.

25 October 1916

Remained in Battery: nothing very exciting: amm waggons stuck in mud in the evening.

We heard that the Kaiser was on our front: also of French success at Douaumont.

26 October 1916

Went to OP: saw one of our aeroplanes shot down near Le Transloy.

27 October 1916

Horrible wet day: remained in Battery playing bridge.

28/29 October 1916

Wet day, & horribly muddy.

30 October 1916

Went off to Amiens with Majors Toppin & Archdale[2] in general's car: for a days joy ride: spent a good deal of money: arrived back at 1.30 a.m. up to our knees in mud.

31 October 1916

Rode up to Bornafay wood: & walked thence to bty position: heard that Marsh[3] had got MC.

1 November 1916

Horrible wet day: condition of dugouts getting bad.

2 November 1916

Another wet day.

3 November 1916

Left at 6 a.m. for front line: got lost in fog & reached Bn HdQrs at 8.30 a.m.: repaired line to Rainbow trench, & waded through mud & water to 'Gusty'. Heavy german fire on most of the day. Saw feeble Hun attack in afternoon: easily stopped. Remained at Bn HdQrs for night with Lincolns (17th Div): very nice people: fresh Hun attack on Zenith[4] heavily repulsed in evening.

4 November 1916

Arrived back at Battery, covered in mud, at 9 a.m.: walked down to Waggon line at 4 p.m. Marsh coming up to Battery.

5 November 1916

Remained in Waggon Line: & heard at 10 p.m. that I was detailed to go for a weeks rest at Mericourt, with 22 men of Brigade.

6 November 1916

Rode down to Mericourt[5] to RA rest billets at the Chateau: nice dry quarters.

7 November 1916

Wet day: went into Corbie in afternoon & had tea.

8 November 1916

Went in & spent the day at Amiens: saw the Cathedral.

9/10 November 1916

Fine day went for a ride: Tea at Heilly.

11 November 1916

Had an easy day of it: Gens Wardrope and Evans[6] came round during morning.

Sunday 12 November 1916
Remained 'easy' most of the day: had tea at Heilly.

13 November 1916
Returned to Meaulte to rejoin Bty: Bde was addressed by

The farm of the former chateau at Mericourt, where Eddie Giffard had a week's rest in November 1916.

Gen Evans: Tomorrow the 61st Bge is dissolved: I go with Left Section to B/75, under Major Archdale: Marsh with Rt Section to Captain McDonald,[7] C/74.

14 November 1916
Am now in B/75. At 3.30 Major Toppin told me to get my leave warrant, & come to Amiens in motor with Colonel Buzzard. Reached Amiens at 6.30 p.m., & had a good dinner at Godfects[8] (at Colonel Buzzard's[9] invitation).

15 November 1916
Left Amiens for Boulogne at 12.15 a.m.: reached Boulogne

at 7 a.m.: left at 1.30 p.m., & reached Folkestone at 3 p.m.:
Victoria 6 p.m.
  Home 10 p.m.

16–26 November 1916
LEAVE.

The following carbon copy of a report by CO 7th Lincs
was found in a pocket of Eddie's notebook:

HeadQtrs
51st Infantry Bde.

Reference the operations in Zenith Sector, I cannot speak
too highly of the general support given to my Battalion
by the Artillery. The curtain of fire set up being such as
to cut off the enemy counterattacking us from all possibility of support, and I should like to specially mention
the FOO Lieut. GIFFARD, to whose observation and
constant and concise reports I was much indebted for
corroborative evidence of the situation in front from
time to time — Communication with the front line being
so difficult, made the reports furnished by Lieut.
GIFFARD all the more valuable.

7–11–16   Signed F. E. METCALFE Lt Col.
              Cmdg. 7th Btln. Lincolnshire Reg.

To OC A/61 B/61 & C/61
              For your information please.

12–11–16   H. Vaughan Lt RFA
              adj. 61st Bde RFA

Sunday 26 November 1916

Left Victoria at 7.50: & reached Folkestone 9.45. Boulogne 12.15 p.m.: losing my breakfast on way over: No train till tomorrow morning. Stayed at Officers' Club.

27 November 1916

Left Boulogne at 11 a.m. and reached Abbeville at 2.30 p.m., where I had to kick my heels, waiting for a train.

28 November 1916

Left at 3 a.m. for Hangest: which I reached at 4 a.m.: slept in RTO's office till daylight: found Battery quite close by: everyone rather disgusted at moving next day, to go into action again: men not rested enough, or horses either.

29 November 1916

Left Hangest at 10.30 a.m. for Argoeuves (via Picquigny & Ailly-sur-Somme), which we reached at 2 p.m.: fair billets: attempt to walk into Amiens, failed, at first milestone.

30 November 1916

Left for Daours at 8.30 a.m.: very cold & raw: reached billets at 12.30 p.m.

1 December 1916

Left for Carnoy at 7 a.m.: stopping at Mericourt[10] on the way: reached Carnoy at 4 p.m.: could not get vehicles up to the Camp, (uphill & through 3 foot of mud): Messcart finally arrived at 1.30 a.m. Uncomfortable day altogether.

2 December 1916

Rather a picnic for breakfast: went to Bde at 9 a.m. with McCracken,[11] & went up with the Colonel to Combles to see new positions: Bty pos which we take over from the

French is at Fregicourt. Very cold but found a nice comfortable mess on return.

3 December 1916

Another cold day: left at 3.30 p.m. for New Bty position with 8 waggons of ammunition: arrived about 7 p.m.: long job getting amm in: 1 horse was killed & 3 wounded: got back at 2.15 a.m. in the morning: bed 3.30 a.m.!

4 December 1916

McCracken & Foley left at 1 p.m. for new Bty position with the right section: mail arrived long overdue.

5 December 1916

Cold rainy day, & all frost in the ground thawing. Williams[12] left at 10 p.m. with the Left section for Fregicourt position: Cake & punch arrived.

6 December 1916

Cold day Easterly wind: prepared to leave about 6 p.m. with Centre section for New Bty position.

Reached position at 9.30 p.m. about. Slept at forward battery position at Fregicourt.

7 December 1916

Remained in battery position all day: very quiet day: cold.

8 December 1916

Another cold & wet day.

9 December 1916

The Major returned: I went off to Bn HdQrs at the Quarries, near Sailly-Saillisel, in evening (2nd G Gds).

Sunday 10 December 1916

Relieved at Bn HdQrs at 7 p.m.: the mud up in the trenches is appalling.

11 December 1916

Walked down to new Bty position in morning: fine cold day.

12 December 1916

Went down to DAC with Foley: very cold snow blizzard during day: walked back most of way & had tea at Brigade. New Bty position has to be found. Received (unexpectedly) nice parcels from Cassilis Red X .

13 December 1916

Remained about Battery. Fine dull day.

14 December 1916

Went to reconnoitre a forward position for Left Section:
    Move to new Bty position again postponed.
    Heard that I am to go shortly to 74th Bge HdQrs (prospective Adjutant to Col Buzzard).[13]

15 December 1916

New Bty position still unsettled: likewise my departure to 74th Bge HdQrs.

16 December 1916

Heard the great news of the French push near 'Verdun'. Went over to 74th Bde HeadQrs (near Ginchy) to try & settle when I should come over: (which was as soon as possible). Rt & centre sections moved in the evening about 400 yds further forward.

17 December 1916

Cold fine day: foggy.

18 December 1916

Cold raw day: went to Bn HdQrs (Quarries) 2nd I Gds.

19 December 1916

Went down Front trench at 4.30 a.m. with Major Grier:[14] returned at 7 a.m.: after breakfast went down to Register guns on front line: returned to Bty at 4 p.m.

20 December 1916

Cold, & hard frost: Left Section attempted to move into their new Forward Position in evening: result, at 10.30 p.m. both guns stuck, one near gun position & one half a mile away.

21 December 1916

Got both guns into position.

22 December 1916

McCracken went to frontline to try & register forward section, but could not make communication all day.

23 December 1916

Major registered forward section: Mess moved to rear position: but I sleep with forward section.

24 December 1916

Remain with Forward Section most of the day, & mess with Battery: half of Xmas hamper arrived.

25 December 1916

Christmas Day: ¼ hours Xmas Strafe for Bosches at 8.30 & 11.30 a.m.: mens rations very bad, especially the plum pudding. Received large letter mail.

26 December 1916

Heavy bombardment on Hun trenches from Noon–4 p.m.: great aeroplane activity.

Byrne[15] came up from WL.

27 December 1916

Very nice sunny day for a change: remainder of hamper arrived!!

28 December 1916

Rain again. Foley arrived back from leave: slept down at rear position, where I continue to for future.

29 December 1916

Rain again: Forward Section started making gun pits proper.

30 December 1916

Fine day: nothing doing.

31 December 1916

Rather wet again: visited Forward Section etc.

1 January 1917

New Year's Day. Went with Hay[16] (of D/76) to look from OP near Morval: & lunched with D/76 on return.

2 January 1917

Went to Bn HdQrs, where 20th Div (SLI) were relieving 2nd I Gds.

3 January 1917

Went up to Sailly-Saillisel to observe & returned to Bty by 4 p.m. (Splitting headache).

4 January 1917

Nothing doing.

5 January 1917

Bright clear day: Huns very active with Aeroplanes & Balloons: heavily shelled valley to right of battery with 5.9" & 4.2" all day.

6 January 1917

Heard that we move shortly: just as we are comfortably settled in!!

7 January 1917

Went down to DAC for a Court Martial: lunching at Waggon Line on way: rode & walked back with Major Hovil:[17] nice fine day.

8 January 1917

Officer of relieving Bty came up in afternoon: 20th Division: very sorry to be leaving our 'comfy' position.

9 January 1917

B/92 relieved us at 2 p.m., taking over our guns complete; rode down to Waggon Line with Major for one night: Cherry Brandy arrived.

10 January 1917

Rode up at 9.30 a.m. to New Bty position, at B5 A3½2½, with two telephonists: only a sergeant to hand over, who knew nothing: no wires to take over, all dugouts under water: & Mess, the only decent place occupied by 86th Bty. Met Major Reid[18] of 127th Bty: (Don Q).

11 January 1917

Major came up early: detachments also with material to

get shelter for the night. Horrible day, cold & sleet showers.

12 January 1917
Nasty cold day, sleet & snow: wretched for men working on dugouts: a fair muddle seems to have been made of 'taking over' lines etc.

13 January 1917
Very cold raw day; met Gen Wardrope at Catacombs in morning: & walked up to Sailly-Saillisel: & then walked back across country to Battery.

14 January 1917
Remained in Battery all day: work on improving position.
Two bottles of 'Menthe Monopole' arrived.

15 January 1917
Cold frosty morning: Williams went away to course at Daours, & Foley returned to Battery.

16 January 1917
Went up to OP, SE of Rancourt, & spent the day there but too foggy to see.

17 January 1916
Woke up to a heavy fall of snow: fairly cold: nothing much doing, beyond a little snowballing!

18 January 1916
A little more snow, & very hazy: but better than rain.

19 January 1916
Ditto: walked up to OP with Sapper officer.

20 January 1917

Went to OP at 8.30 a.m.: rather a lot of hostile shelling: a few 4.2" fell near Bty position: & OP trench not too pleasant: relieved midday by Foley.

21 January 1917

Still frosty: went to Bn HdQrs in evening: 3rd GGs: the Major went Home on leave.

22 January 1917

Went up to OP with Captain Denton, but light very bad all day: McCracken turned up in evening to assume command.

23 January 1917

Hard frost: remained in Battery: D/76 heavily shelled.

24 January 1917

Hard frost again: nice day, but not much doing: Byrne returned from Leave.

26 January 1917

Spent the afternoon at OP: very cold wind.

27 January 1917

Attack by 29th Div[19] at 5.30 a.m., apparently quite successful: 350 prisoners. Kaiser's birthday present.

28 January 1917

Went up to OP for the morning: & to Bn HdQrs (4th G Gds) (Colonel Hamilton)[20] in evening. Very cold again: Watts[21] joined Battery.

29 January 1917

Very nice winter's day: Hun fairly active.

30 January 1917

Attempting to snow: went to OP in afternoon: very cold.

31 January 1917

More snow during the night.

1 February 1917

Went to OP early: heavy Hun strafe near Priez Farm: damage nil.

2 February 1917

Weather still the same: remained in Battery: Mince pies, & pyjamas arrived. Huns heavily bombarded near Sailly.

3 February 1917

Extra hard frost: fairly quiet day.

4 February 1917

Walked down to Waggon Line with Foley: heard of success near Serre[22] (200 prisoners).

5 February 1917

OP: quiet day: heard of Anzac's push[23] of previous night.

6 February 1917

Remained near Battery: had tea with Foley at GDA.
America breaks off Dip relations with Germany:[24] very cold wind.

7 February 1917

Went to OP at midday.

8 February 1917

7.30 a.m. 17th Div attacked at Saillisel: apparently objective gained. Gramophone arrived at last.

9 February 1917

Fairly quiet: a few 5.9" in vicinity of battery. Went to Bn HdQrs 1st G Gds (Major Vaughan)[25] in evening. Leave suspended.

10 February 1917

Rather a heavy cold: uneventful day: smell of gas in evening.

11 February 1917

Went to OP early: nice 'warm' sunny day: heard about Croix de Guerre.[26] Hun unusually quiet.

12 February 1917

Rather warmer, but only thawed a little: visited 74th Bde HdQrs.

13 February 1917

Thawed a good deal during the day: went to OP for afternoon: big strafe on Hun trenches.

14 February 1917

Nice day again: walked down to Maurepas with Foley: rest of the day quiet!

15 February 1917

Big strafe by 15th Corps: fine and warmer: thawed during day: walked down to GDA in afternoon with McCracken.

16 February 1917

At 5 a.m. Plateau Amm Dump fired by German bomb: explosions occurred all day.

Warmer & attempted to rain.

17 February 1917

Motored down to 4th Army HdQrs, Querrieu, & received

medal from General Nivelle. Had dinner at GDA on way back: heavy rain in evening.

18 February 1917

Foggy day: & mild: very quiet.

19 February 1917

Foggy all day & quiet; went up to OP for morning.

20 February 1917

Very wet, & muddy, but warm. Frost is certainly better than this. Heard that prisoners at Baillescourt[27] (Ancre) were 773 (12 officers).

21 February 1917

Very foggy: & warm. Went to Bn HdQrs in evening 2nd G Gds (Colonel de Crespigny).[28]

22 February 1917

Very foggy, & quiet: still no news of leave.

23 February 1917

Very thick fog: OP all day: mud appalling.

24 February 1917

Dull foggy: walked down to Waggon Line with McCracken, in afternoon: rode back.

25 February 1917

Went to OP at midday.

26 February 1917

Heard definitely that I go to A/75 as Acting Capt.[29] News of probable German retirement to 'Hindenburg' Line: several villages evacuated North of the Ancre.

27 February 1917

Fine day: remained in Battery.

28 February 1917

5.25 a.m. 29th Div made attack at Sailly-Saillisel, & gained all objectives: 60 prisoners. As German retirement seems quite 'on the cards', leave is rather doubtful.

1 March 1917

Nice drying day: went to OP: Hun planes rather in evidence.

2 March 1917

Remained in Battery: Bdr Matthews wounded, while we were testing new signalling apparatus.

3 March 1917

Foggy morning: heavy strafe by 15th Corps in afternoon, preparatory to attack on following morning.

Sunday 4 March 1917

Frost again: fine bright day: attack of 15th Corps successful: 100 odd prisoners. Lachrimatory shell scattered in neighbourhood in evening.

5 March 1917

More snow: Byrne came up to Battery, & I went down to waggon line to stay in evening.

6 March 1917

Frosty & cold: remained in WL.

7 March 1917

Strong & bitter cold wind. Rode up to Battery in afternoon: heard Byrne had departed. Walked back after tea & had dinner with Hancock[30] & David.[31]

8 March 1917

Rose at 6.15 a.m. (3rd morning in succession) very cold wind: McCracken had lunch with me.

9 March 1917

Another very cold day with snow & sleet: still no water in the troughs: a few HV gun shell fell near Maricourt.

10 March 1917

Heard I was promoted acting Captain: going later to A/75. Rode up to Bty in evening & had dinner & walked back.

Sunday 11 March 1917

Nice warm day: remained about Waggon Line all day: dined with D/75.

   act. Captain dates from 18/2/17.

12 March 1917

Fair amount of rain during the night: warmer so rode up to Bty in afternoon, & walked back: New sub, Porter[32] by name, joined: Heard of Capture of Bagdad.[33]

13 March 1917

Not much news: but air rather full of rumours of Boche Withdrawal.

14 March 1917

Batteries of 75th Bge preparing to move forward: 1200 rds of amm moved to a more forward position: lot of rain during the day.

15 March 1917

Fine drying day: walked up to Battery in morning: saw forward position. Huns certainly appear withdrawing on our front. Rode back to waggon line for tea.

16 March 1917

Cold foggy morning. Expecting to move Battery forward any moment.

17 March 1917

BAPAUME captured 7.00 a m. Sent off 6 teams to move guns to new position early: rode up to Battery at 9 a.m.: stopped there all day & moved last 3 guns forward in evening. Dined with McCracken and walked back to WL, calling in at Brigade on way.

18 March 1917

Remained in WL: had dinner at HdQrs Mess, & had a Gramaphone concert.

19 March 1917

Rather a cold wind: rode up at midday to new Bty position with Padre: Bosch going back all along the line: unable to pursue him properly on account of bad, or rather no roads, across the respective front lines. Walked back to Battery, having tea at Bde HdQrs on the way.

20 March 1917

Foul day: cold wind, rain sleet & snow!
Bad pursuing weather.[34]

21 March 1917

Started at 7.15 a.m. riding to Bty position; very cold wind, but drying day. Rode through St Pierre Vaust [?] wood, round south of Vaux, & along Canal du Nord to Moislains; thence to Nurlu & back through Manancourt & Gov Farm. Country nice & dry towards Nurlu. Boches burning villages at leisure, as we at present can get no guns up to them: very annoying.

22 March 1917

Another cold day with snow showers. Brigade are apparently coming out to rest any day now.

23 March 1917

Frost, & cold windy day. No definite news of coming out, but apparently in 2 or 3 days.

24 March 1917

Very sharp frost, & cold windy day. Summer Time starts 11 p.m. tonight, which becomes midnight.

25 March 1917

Sunny day & warmer: rode up to Bty, & had lunch there.
    At 11 p.m. summer time commenced.

26 March 1917

74th Bde marched out to rest: very wet day: Dined with P. McCormick[35] at Maricourt.

27 March 1917

Left at 7.45 a.m. (very cold) to take Pack horses up to collect ammunition near Bouleaux Wood & Morval: went back to waggon line to Lunch.

28 March 1917

Hard frost again: McCracken & Foley came down in afternoon, expect to move out in 2 days.

29 March 1917

Horrible wet day: Guns came down at Midday. Preparations for moving to Morlancourt the next day.

30 March 1917

The whole Battery left at 10 a.m. for Morlancourt, which

we reached at 2 p.m.: Good horse lines & fair billets. Concerts every night.

31 March 1917

In afternoon joined A/75, Major Corbett[36] coming over to 'B': weather bad.

Sunday 1 April 1917

Went to Church in morning. Storms all day, & v windy. Dined at B/75 in evening.

2 April 1917

Usual -- weather. Concert in evening at 9 p.m., at which the General performed.

3 April 1917

Very windy, & hard frost, but not drying up much.

4 April 1917

Vile day with snow: usual evening concert the one redeeming feature, & America's entry into war.[37]

5 April 1917

Fine day at last: General went round Billets etc. Boxing Competition at 1.30. At 3.30 p.m., went for a short flight in a B25[38] (Peter) Pilot Breakall[39] C Flight No 9 Squadron: enjoyed it very much.

6 April 1917

Another fine day: General Fielding[40] inspected Waggon Lines etc.

7 April 1917

Gen Wardrop expected, but did not turn up: 74th Bde officers beat 75th at soccer.

8 April 1917

Easter Sunday. Church Parade: had a ride in afternoon, &
tea'd at 'B' Bty. Nice fine day.

9 April 1917

Snow shower during the morning, but cleared up in evening.
Heard first news of the VIMY offensive:[41] 4000–5000
prisoners.

10 April 1917

Snow showers. Gen Wardrope inspected the Lines. Offensive going strong: over 10,000 prisoners, & many guns:
advance reached 4 miles in depth.

11 April 1917

75th Bde defeated 74th at Rugger: snow again in evening:
concert 9 p.m.

12 April 1917

Cold day again: snowed in afternoon, as per usual.

13 April 1917

Fine day: drying up.

14 April 1917

Fine sunny day: 1st & 3rd Army offensives[42] going on successfully.

Sunday 15 April 1917

Church in the morning: rather wet again.

16 April 1917

Fine morning: rain again as per usual in afternoon. Heard of
big Hun Counter Attack between NOREUIL & HERMIES
repulsed with heavy losses.

17 April 1917

Very cold wind, & rain. Heard of big French success[43] between Soissons & Rheims, with over 10,000 Prisoners.

18 April 1917

Raining again: went with Foley & had a bath at Ville.

19 April 1917

Fine day: warmer: skeleton driving drills near Bois de Taille: preparing for Sports.

20 April 1917

Fine sunny day at last: Sports came off in afternoon. Patronized by Lord Cavan,[44] Gens Wardrope, Ponsonby[45] & P of W.[46]

21 April 1917

Fine again: played in Rugby Football match in afternoon.

Sunday 22 April 1917

Nice fine day. Rode over to Heilly & had tea.

23 April 1917

Fine sunny: dined with 'B' Battery.

24 April 1917

Left at 8.30 a.m. with firing battery for Calibration near Assevillers. Nice sunny day again.

25 April 1917

Still fine.

26 April 1917

Went to Ville with Major Porter for a bath.

27 April 1917

Drill order at Bois de Taille, with the CO.

28 April 1917

Fine day again: Bty staff ride in morning.

Sunday 29 April 1917

Drill Order, & preparations for the 'Test' following day.

30 April 1917

Two Bdes tested by Gen Wardrope for coming into action, open fighting.

1 May 1917

Nice warm day. Left at 7 a.m. with guns for Assevillers, for Calibration with NCT.[47]

2 May 1917

Warm spring day: half holiday.

3 May 1917

Nice weather still. Drill Order.

4 May 1917

Battery staff ride in morning: first news of further attack on 'Hindenburg Line', capture of Bullecourt & Fresnoy.

5 May 1917

Very warm: thundery all afternoon.

Sunday 6 May 1917

Nice fine day, cool, half holiday, & Bty football match.

7 May 1917

Warm, sunny day. GOCRA of 4th Army[48] made rapid inspection of GDA: rain in evening.

8 May 1917

Fine again: Sports on following day put off suddenly, moving somewhere (?). Ypres appears most popular choice. Dined at Bde HdQrs.

9 May 1917

Fine again: no 'official' news of move, but we do move on Friday 11th: up North.[49]

10 May 1917

Fine morning: preparing for move on following day: entraining at 'Heilly'.

11 May 1917

Reveille 4.30 a.m.: Left Morlancourt for Heilly at 8 a.m.: left Heilly in train 2 p.m. Hot day: arrived St Omer midnight.

12 May 1917

Marched for Campagne, where we arrived 5 a.m. Water & fed: & rested till 11 a.m.: very hot day: everyone a bit tired.

Sunday 13 May 1917

30 years of age today!! Major Hovil returned in evening from leave, & took over command of Battery at 9.30 p.m.

14 May 1917

Fine day: remained in Battery.

15 May 1917

Rode into St Omer in afternoon, with Foley & Williams: cooler day: but still fine.

16 May 1917

Quiet day in the Lines.

17 May 1917

Wet day: nothing much doing, beyond Battery drill etc: more birthday mail.

Russian situation[50] appears rather critical.

18 May 1917

Gundrill in morning: rode into St Omer with the Major, & walked back along the canal.

Italians take 3375 prisoners.[51]

19 May 1917

Harness inspection: ride round in afternoon.

Sunday 20 May 1917

Another hot day: Church parade, open air service at Chateau.

Heard that we move Eastwards on Tuesday.

21 May 1917

Heard that we probably go into Action shortly at Hill 53, near Messines:[52] in 2nd ANZAC Corps.

Major offered bet of 20/= to 10/= that War is not over by 1/1/18: which I took!

Walked into Argues with Major, & did a little shopping.

22 May 1917

Reveille 4 a.m.: Marched at 8 a.m. for Strazeele, via Renescure, Ebblinghem & Haazebrouck. Arrived in billets at 3 p.m.: quite comfortable: but wet march.

23 May 1917

Fine day: grazed horses, & prepared to March the next day for new Waggon Lines near Bailleul.

24 May 1917

Marched at 8.30 a.m. for new Waggon Lines, 4 Kilometres

East of Bailleul. Got in at 1 p.m. Very little accommodation, but fine. Attached to 25th Division for the Push.

25 May 1917
Rode into Bailleul with Major; had tea & remained in to Dinner with Major Denton, at Officers' Club. Great 'preparations going on' behind our Lines here: numbers of heavy guns etc.

26 May 1917
Went up early with all Amm Waggons to Forward Waggon Lines WNW of Neuve Eglise: left 6.30 a.m., arrived in 9 a.m.: rode back later to old Lines, where guns still remain. 30 men remain up at Battery position for working on it: fairly near front Line (800 yds).

27 May 1917
Whit Sunday. Another hot summer day. Had a party of Anzacs in morning for working on road. Saw two occupants of Kite Balloon parachute down after being shelled by Bosh.

28 May 1917
Went up to Bty position with Major, & thence on to forward WL (Mobile) getting back to Immobile WL at 2 p.m.

29 May 1917
Went up again to Bty position: cooler day.

30 May 1917
Rode up to By position with Major, & on to forward Waggon Line, which had been shelled the previous evening: horses had stampeded, & many stayed away; got back to Immobile Waggon Line at 2.45 p.m.

Ordered up by Colonel to go up to Mobile Waggon Lines, & take charge. All horses were moved out at 8 p.m., away from shelled area for night. I remained in wagon Line for night, with Guards of Batteries.

31 May 1917

Disturbed at 3 a.m. by sound of shells whistling over: 4 a.m. they fell rather close to tent, so got up & walked out, & collected the guards, to make for a safer place. D/75 Amm Waggon hit, & one limber blown up: two other waggons on fire: with Cpl S/S[53] & much trepidation, put two buckets of water on fire: & soon put it right out: 8 or 9 waggons damaged. Met area Commandant at 10.30 a.m., & chose new waggon lines at S 12 a 77. Moved over with bde in afternoon.

1 June 1917

Went in morning to reconnoitre new roads to gun position. & rode down to Immobile waggons in evening.

2 June 1917

Rode in to Bailleul in afternoon for shopping etc & called at Immobile Waggon Lines on way back.

Sunday 3 June 1917

Went up to gun position in morning: all guns now in position. Heavy bombardment of Messines & vicinity during the day. Part of preliminary bombardment(?). Opinions differ as to whether this is to be a very big push or only local. Enormous numbers of guns in position. Church Service in afternoon.

4 June 1917

Rode down to Immobile WL & on to Connaught Rd to see Clay model of hostile front. We have fatigue parties at all hours of day & night.

5 June 1917

German Aeroplane set fire to Amm dump near Bailleul, at 8.45 a.m.: many violent explosions during next 3 hours. Some of our Batteries (GDA) appear to be having rather a rough time: B/74 having 4500 rds blown up.

6 June 1917

Bombardment all day preparing for attack tomorrow. Hun a bit more active, evidently 'tumbling' to it. Went up to OP with Major in afternoon to register guns on MESSINES ridge: light bad: walked back across country to waggon lines, very thirsty on return at 8.15 p.m. 3 horses killed, 1 wounded.

7 June 1917

The DAY.[54] 3.30 a.m. Violent Bombardment & some mines blown up. All of us waiting news of the attack: the usual rumours going about. Rode up to Battery position, & walked back via Group. No definite news in: but all appears well.

8 June 1917

Still no definite news of extent of success. Rode up to Battery, & walk with Major to the new OP, near Huns farm: guns registered. Capture of guns rather disappointing so far.

9 June 1917

Remained about waggon lines. Expecting to move out of action soon. Heavy enemy counter attack in evening, which we heard afterwards, was heavily repulsed.

10 June 1917

Moved down to Immobile Waggon Lines: Guns came out in evening. Bty Casualties in action 9 men wounded.

11 June 1917

Bde marched at 11 a.m. for billets at Pradelle: quite comfortable billets, & good horse lines.

12 June 1917

Very warm morning: Thundershowers in afternoon, which did a lot of good. From further information, the Messines affair seems to have been a great success in every way. We expect to move North soon, 5th Army, taking over from Ypres to sea (?).

13 June 1917

Felt a bit queer in the morning, & stopped work after Stables. Rested all the afternoon: Tummy very nasty.

14 June 1917

Uncomfortable night & felt very weak all day: seems like Ptomaine poisoning: feeding only on water & milk.

15 June 1917

Still feeling a wreck, & very weak. Tummy a little better in afternoon.

16 June 1917

Battery left at 9.30 a.m. for HERZEELE: I remained behind with Gamble[55] to help me, to recuperate, & avoid if possible going into Hospital: probably get special Leave warrant on 19th: hope I am fit to travel by then.

17 June 1917

Not feeling up to much, but am trying to sit up for a bit to prepare for moving.

18 June 1917

Bad night & little rest; felt slightly better in the morning.

Weather still very hot; wish it would turn cooler for a day or two!

Got a little cooler during evening.

19 June 1917

A better night & much cooler morning. Feeling a little stronger, but not easy to get any suitable food beyond eggs & milk. Kane[56] arrived at 7 p.m. with mail & Leave Warrant for 23rd! So leave here on 22nd. Feeling better. Major Mockett brought me some soups.[57]

20 June 1917

More rain & cool morning. Feeling on the mend. Had a little walk outside: rather boring work with nothing to read.

21 June 1917

Nice cool morning. Went for promenade outside: & felt the better for it. Waddell[58] arrived unexpectecily at 1.15 p.m., with my horses, & so I quickly dressed, & we caught the 4 p.m. train at Hazebrouck, reached Boulogne at 8.30 p.m. travelling in Luggage Van. Enjoyed a decent feed, Champagne, & hot bath, & felt better.

22 June 1917

Went on board the *Onward* at 10 a.m., sailed at 11.10 a.m.

reached	Folkestone	1 p.m.
	Victoria	3.15 p.m.
	Marlborough	7.30 p.m.

[This notebook ends with a list of points for some military occasion, and notes of music available on records, thus:]

1. Harness: oiling of.
2. Battery Staff: details of.
3. Petrol tins: plugs.

4. Gas drill.
5. Buckets.
6. Trumpeter Dunn (removal of Trumpets).
7. QMS to indent for Connectors, limbering up. Vide GRO
   592 page 87 of Part 11 GROs.

Gramophone Records

A Summer Cycle (London
  Ronald [?])
Bacarolle
Druids Prayer
Liebestraume

Indian Love Lyrics
Rubinstein's Melody in 'F'
Valse Septembre
Rachmaninoff (South
  Corps[?] Military Band).

6

Eddie's Diary: The Fourth Notebook

Fourth Return from Leave

Saturday 7 July 1917

Left Victoria 7.50 a.m.: Folkestone 10.20 a.m. Arrived Boulogne 12 midday. Heard of air raid on London.[1] Slept at Officers' Club.

Sunday 8 July 1917

Left at 4 a.m. by train for Poperinghe: stopped at Haze-brouck from 11 a.m. till 4.36: reached Poperinghe at 6.15 p.m.: went to GDA 75th Brigade still at Herzeele: coming up on 10th: remain in Poperinghe to meet them.

9 July 1917

Remained at Poperinghe. Lunch at GDA: heard that Battery moves into action on night of 11th & that, as Maj. Hovil goes to Bde, I shall command Bty in action.

10 July 1917

Made my way to waggon lines at S 28 B Central: & met Bty, who had just come in.

11 July 1917

Rode up, & walked to Bty position at 10 a.m. with Major and Davies[2] and walked back. Heard of further Russian successes.[3] Battery went up into action in evening, under Davies and Waddell:[4] 1 Dvr wounded, & 4 horses. Preparations going forward for, apparently, a very big push: Huns have quite a number of HV Guns.

12 July 1917

Remained in Waggon Lines: heard of our reverse at Nieuport[5] and Russian further successes. Had dinner with McCracken.[6]

13 July 1917

Rode up partly & walked to Battery: heard definitely that I go up shortly to command Bty, whilst Major commands Brigade. Dvr Camps died of wounds. Hot day, walked back to Waggon Line.

14 July 1917

A few thunder showers: a warm SH day.[7] Gun Limbers etc., comprising Immobile Waggon Lines, moved in afternoon to Herzeele. Part of lost ground at Nieuport reported retaken.

15 July 1917

Went up to Bty position & lunched there: Seward[8] came back with me to take over the Waggon Lines.

16 July 1917

Went up early to Battery to take over command, whilst Major commands brigade.

17 July 1917

Went down to OP (K 22) in morning: intense bombardment

continues: during night Hun was very obnoxious with his gas shells: masks on.

18 July 1917

Went down to Group HdQrs in morning: wet day. A bit headachy after gas of previous night. Waddell went down to detached section.

19 July 1917

Bombardment continues fairly intensively: the Hun does not reply as much as one would expect.

20 July 1917

McFadzean [*sic*][9] returned from leave: warmish day again.

Sunday 22 July 1917

Bombardment continues. German aeroplane driven down by 2 French planes near front line.

23 July 1917

Very much annoyed through the night by Mustard oil & other concoctions of Hun gas shell: Gaspirators on most of the night: also a good deal of 5.9" & 4.2". Hun evidently very windy about being attacked.

24 July 1917

During the night gas shells again came over: Bosch puts down barrage regularly every morning now, just before dawn: anticipating attack by us. Walked down to Waggon Line with Major Hovil:[10] very 'SH' day.[11]

25 July 1917

Enemy put fairly heavy fire up all night: but luckily no gas shell, & so we were not disturbed much. Nice drop of rain in morning. Registered one gun in evening. Practised Barrage with 'Gaspirators'.

26 July 1917

Hun was very annoying during night, putting 4" gun shells round us: fairly quiet during the day. Offensive supposed to be postponed for a day or two?

27 July 1917

Quiet night. Heard during afternoon that Huns had vacated front line [trenches?]: our own Infantry & French occupied them during evening.

28 July 1917

No further advance during the day:[12] heavy artillery fire at 9 p.m.: & gas shell over, which necessitated gaspirators on.

29 July 1917

Wet day & quiet on the whole from our point of view.

30 July 1917

Y Day: Bosch very quiet but ourselves & French very noisy.

31 July 1917

Zero day: 3.50 a.m. attack began: very little opposition apparently. Barrage fire considered very good by Infantry. Went up with Major Hovil, Corbett, Denton & Seigne to look for new Battery Positions.[13] No definite news of extent of success, on other fronts. Huns appear to have retired in some disorder. Heard that 74th Bde had had 4 officers killed — Vaughan, Harris (Doctor), Wise & Scot [?] Deakin: very bad luck: Ireland and Taylor wounded.[14] Some of RHA crossed the canal.

1 August 1917

Appalling wet day: which is spoiling offensive. Dugout beginning to collapse.

2 August 1917

Still firing at long range: too muddy to move. Rotten bad luck, being unable to follow up initial success of offensive.

3 August 1917

Horrible wet day: attempted to build new Gun Position across canal: rather heartbreaking in the rain.

4 August 1917

Still showery; but drying up slightly: made Platforrns for Gun Pits & erected Camouflage.

5 August 1917

Fine day again: further work on new position: Hun rather unpleasant at times. Aeroplanes & artillery generally very active: a lot of firing all night.

6 August 1917

Another fine day: had amm. taken to new position, in readiness.

7 August 1917

Sudden orders at 11 a.m. to move to new position in the evening. Moved out at 5 p.m., & got in action by 6.30 p.m.: quite a comfortable move in.

8 August 1917

Went up to Fourche farm to reregister guns, with Major Corbett[15] & Seigne:[16] good view of country: Hun rather nasty in evening, putting 5.9" uncomfortably near.

9 August 1917

Went to FOURCHE FARM[17] again, to do some firing. Had tea at Brigade.

10 August 1917

Remained in Battery. Bosche turned on 8", 5.9", on to Canal from Boesinghe Pontoon to Crapouillets Pontoon, from 7 p.m. to 9 p.m. Battery position shelled intermittently during night, with 77 mms.

11 August 1917

Went up to Fourche Farm to do a little firing: communications being bad, had a disappointing morning: 7.15 p.m., Bosche turned on 8", 5.9" 77 mms onto Canal & searching back, as far as Battery: had to clear position till 10.30 p.m. Dinner all went west, no casualties, luckily. F sub dugout[18] blown in for second time.

12 August 1917

Went up to Fourche Farm, but retired again as Hun had got it set: went to Wood 16 and did a little firing from there. Quiet night for a change.

13 August 1917

Went with McFadzean to establish new OP: a healthier place than Fourche Farm. Fairly quiet all day, but canal was heavily shelled from 6.30 p.m. till 8.30. Some gas shell during the night.

14 August 1917

Fairly quiet on the whole. Bosch planes very active during afternoon, having things more or less their own way.

15 August 1917

'Y' day; preparing Barrage tables for the next day.

Bosch very quiet: probably withdrawing guns, or trying to.

16 August 1917

Intense gas shell & heavy bornbardment by our own guns all night: 4.45 a.m. attack[19] commenced: very intense bombardments: Bosch reply appears very feeble. Attack on XIVth Corps Front completely successful: Barrage again thought much of: advance only about 1,000 yds on our front. Bosch naval guns worried us considerably from 7 p.m.–8.30 p.m.

17 August 1917

A few shell dropped about Battery at 4 a.m., as per usual: 8.30 a.m. 5.9" began to fall in vicinity of canal, & near Brigade positions: evidently trying to stop traffic.

18 August 1917

Went down to OP near Sentier Farm, with Seigne, & registered Battery afresh. 9 p.m., 5.9" began to fall in vicinity of Brigade: rather unpleasant for an hour & a half, 'B' battery having gun damaged.

19 August 1917

At 4.45 a.m. assisted in attack by XVIIIth Corps. Went down with Seigne to reconnoitre the country the other side of WIJDENDRIFT. Appears practically impassible for artillery: one mass of Crump holes, & nearly under water. 5 p.m. Brigade positions were rather heavily shelled by 8" & 5.9" till 7.30 p.m.: 2 dugouts blown in & some amm & Camouflage destroyed: fortunately no casualties to Battery: men behaved well: a few showing the strain a bit.

20 August 1917

Fairly quiet day & night.

21 August 1917

Went down to Bn HdQrs, & then to OP to register. Quite a warm day, quiet on the whole. Major Blumenthal[20] joined 'B' Battery temporarily. 11 p.m. gas shell began to fall.

22 August 1917

From 1 a.m.–4 a.m. gaspirators had to be worn, gas shell, & some HE, falling round like rifle bullets. Luckily no casualties: the worst 'gassing' that we have had. Rode down to Waggon Line for day.

23 August 1917

Quiet night for a change: weather looks worse again. At 3.45 p.m. 5.9" again began to fall near Brigade positions, & continued till 5.45 p.m. We fortunately escaped casualties, but 'D' sub gun burnt & both wheels destroyed. 'B' and 'C' had 7 casualties.

24 August 1917

Quiet night again! 9 a.m. heavy stuff began to fall again: from 11 a.m.–3 p.m. they fell fairly intensely, & 'A' subgun practically destroyed. Sergeant Hicks & Bdr Tomkinson wounded, & a Gr slightly wounded: Bosch getting a decided nuisance!

25 August 1917

Quiet night: but from 10 a.m. onwards till 4.30 p.m. 5.9" & 8" fell very continuously all round, & position evacuated for 2 hours: 'B' evacuate their position and take new one.

Sunday 26 August 1917

Quiet night again: a few heavy shell near in the morning: 3 p.m.–8 p.m. a heavy fire from all calibres especially 5.9" & 8" fell over brigade positions & large number of other batteries in vicinity: 7.30 p.m. Staff Sergeant Fitter Cockran killed: turned into a wet night: two more dugouts (fortunately vacated) blown in during afternoon.

27 August 1917

A few heavy shell came over during morning: Cpl Hiscocks unfortunately killed. 1.55–5.26 p.m. assisted in operations on right: Hun put down a fairly heavy barrage from Wood 14 to the railway, of 4.1" & 5.9": rather nerve-racking at the Battery, Waddell having one shell 6 yds away: however, no casualties. Horrible wet night & gale of wind.

28 August 1917

Great gale of wind & very muddy: quiet morning, but from 4 p.m. till 8 p.m. 5.9" again fell unpleasantly near.

29 August 1917

Another rotten windy, showery day: fairly quiet, with the exception of a few 5.9"s in the morning: quiet day.

30 August 1917

Huns shelled Canal bank with 8" or 11", most of the day: went down with Seigne to Bn HdQrs & towards front line: quiet night again.

31 August 1917

Went down to OP to register: Hun was unpleasant from Noon onwards putting shrapnel & 4.2"s over near Battery: 3.45 p.m.–5.45 p.m., intense bombardment of Brigade Positions with 8", 5.9": very unpleasant for the time being. 7.45 p.m.–8.45 p.m., Hun very intensely bombarded Bde & neighbouring Bty Positions and Boesinghe Pontoon, with all Calibres, up to 11": most unpleasant, but fortunately we only had two men wounded in Battery: 'a proper hate'.

1 September 1917

A quiet night: & quite quiet all day: the first quiet day for some time.

2 September 1917

Went up to see new Battery Positions in front of Abre Wood: with Seigne, & on to OP to do some firing: went down to Brigade in evening (Gouvy Farm).

3 September 1917

Bosch started to be nasty at 12.30 p.m.: continued intermittently throughout afternoon, culminating in a big Hate from 8 p.m. till 10 p.m.: Irish Guards got some casualties near battery: most of the Field dressings in the battery were used to help them, & also we helped to carry them to Dressing Station: Bosch continued 'pipsqueaking' all night. Tea & Dinner went west.

4 September 1917

Beautiful September day: walked round with Major to Steenbeck Positions & back via OP. Bosch again somewhat unpleasant from 6 p.m.–7.30 p.m.

5 September 1917

Fairly quiet on the whole, but Bosch made himself unpleasant at times: fair night.

6 September 1917

XVIIIth Corps made an attack at 7.30 a.m; we assisted with small barrage. Went down to WIJDENDRIFT to call on Bn Cmdr (Colonel Follett,[21] 2nd Coldstreams) with Seward.[22] As we were leaving, a pipsqueak aircrump burst near us: Seward getting a nice 'blighty' in the thigh: received a glancing wound below right shoulder myself; took Seward to Sentier Farm, whence he was taken by Trolley to

BOESINGHE. Registered guns at OP & returned home. Had Tea at Brigade. Hun began to make himself objectionable at 7.30 p.m.: from 8.30 p.m. to 10 p.m. Bty was intensely bombarded by heavy stuff: most unpleasant. 11.15 p.m.–1.15 a.m. again rather heavily shelled: probably about 600 rds in all fell: very trying to the nerves!

7 September 1917

Felt very sleepy in the morning after our disturbed night. Fortunately a quiet day: went on strengthening Funk holes etc.

8 September 1917

Quiet night, but heard that Waggon Lines had been bombed: Edwards & Jenkins killed:[23] & we had 4 men killed & 8 wounded: shocking bad luck. Attended burial in afternoon at CANADA FARM: & went on to Waggon Line: Bosch strafed us at battery again from 10.45 p.m.–11.15 p.m.

9 September 1917

Quiet day on the whole. Registered guns again in evening.

10 September 1917

Quiet night: went down to WIJDENDRIFT in morning to Bn HdQrs, 3rd G Gds. Had tea at Bde HdQrs: & a hot bath!

11 September 1917

Quiet morning, but at 2 p.m. 5.9" Aircrumps began to fall, followed by a heavy bombardment of Bty position. Gr Hartly badly wounded. Intermittent fire till 6.30 p.m., & 8.30–9.30 p.m. followed by

12 September 1917

Intense Gas shell bombardment from 2 a.m.–5 a.m.: then stood to on SOS[24] till 6.15 a.m. Fairly quiet day on the whole, but 5.9" fell in close proximity, intermittently during afternoon. All sorts of rumours about going out, but we probably stay in till about 21st.

13 September 1917
Rather a heavy bombardment between 3 a.m. & 4 a.m.: fired on SOS for a while: much cooler day.

14 September 1917
Fine day: went down to Bn HdQrs, 2nd Irish Guards, who on night of 13th had 120 casualties, including 80 missing! A sad affair.

15 September 1917
Remained in Bty all day. Five 8" delayed action fell in Battery during afternoon: huge craters made, sides of E & F subs[25] blown in: otherwise no damage. A good deal of shelling during the night.

16 September 1917
4.45 a.m.–6.30 a.m. fired 400 rds on SOS lines: heavy losses inflicted on enemy by all accounts: 5.9" fell uncomfortably near Bty whilst firing, but men stood it well (& Waddell). Davies returned from leave.

17 September 1917
Went down to OP in morning to do a bit of registering: & to Brigade in afternoon, where I stopped for the night, & had an undisturbed sleep: another attack impending!

18 September 1917
Quiet day on the whole: nothing much doing: Seigne went to receive his Croix de Guerre.

19 September 1917

'Y' Day. Preliminary bombardment started at 3 a.m. Nice fine day. 7.30 p.m.–9 p.m. Bosch began to shell vicinity of Bty rather heavily with 4.2" & 4.1" Gun: after which a quiet night.

20 September 1917

5 a.m. got up to prepare for attack: 5.40 a.m. bombardment commenced: our Division does not advance. Fairly quiet for us all day: operations appear to have been quite successful, 1,000 yds advance on 10 mile front. Heard that we go out to rest on 22nd: 3 more Military Medals for battery: Drage, Moore, Fowell.

21 September 1917

Walked down to Bde HdQrs in morning & had lunch: & back to Bty in afternoon: Major Eggleton came in in evening to see about taking over the guns on following morning. 7 p.m. Bosch began to put a nasty Barrage down between Bridge Street & Steam Mill: 7.35 p.m. 5.9" arrived at side of Mess, blowing Sgt Spencer about 6 yds & wounding him in leg: got a cut & bruise behind right ear myself & bled a bit: Mess stores went sky high. Walked down to Bde & got dressed by Cockcroft:[26] then went on to No. 4 CCS, via Bluet Farm & Canada Farm.

22 September 1917

Arrived at No. 4 CCS at 12.30 a.m.: got into a comfortable bed, between sheets, & rather enjoyed the contrast. Visited by Foley, Porter & Martin.[27] Left No. 4 CCS by train at 5 p.m.: Col Bethell[28] came to see me there before I left, & very kindly said that he would try & keep my place for me.

23 September 1917

Arrived at Camiers (near Etaples) at 6 a.m. after a record journey of 13 hrs (70 miles?). Went to comfortable bed at 20th General Hospital: remained there all day, & heard I was a case for Blighty: very comfortable here.

24 September 1917

7 a.m. prepared to leave for Blighty, by putting extra clothes on: left Camiers at 11.15 p.m. [*sic*] arriving Calais 2 p.m. (16 miles). Left Calais, & reached Dover at 5.30 p.m. (English Winter Time). Were there held by hostile air raid[29] till about 11 p.m.

25 September 1917

Left by train about 1.30 a.m., reaching Charing X 4 a.m.: told off to P of W's Hospital Marylebone. Quite a comfortable place (Hotel Great Central). Maudie[30] came and saw me in the afternoon.

[A handwritten copy of the following letter, possibly made by Eddie's father, was found in this notebook.]

12th October 1917

Dear Giffard

Many thanks for your letter ... [reference omitted]. We will do everything possible to get you back when you are fit to come. You have had a very hard time & got hit twice, & you have done damned well, & I greatly appreciate the way in which you commanded & kept A/75 together under very trying conditions.

Yrs ever

(signed) A. Bethell
Colonel RFA

30 November 1917

Left Victoria 7.35 a.m., reaching Folkestone 9.25 a.m. Left for Boulogne 1.30 p.m.: met Colonel Stallard[31] on board. May[32] met me on the Quay & we spent the evening together: saw May off at 9 p.m.

1 December 1917

Left B at 7.30 a.m., travelling up with Colonel Arden,[33] myself for GDA. Reached Amiens at Noon: spent afternoon there, had a shave & did 'some shopping'. Left at 6 p.m. reaching Albert at 7.30 p.m.: stayed at Officers Club the night.

2 December 1917

Left Albert for Buire at 8 a.m.: stayed 3 hours there, bitterly cold: reached Plateau at 2 p.m.; left for Fins at 4 p.m., & arrived 7 p.m.: RTO knew nothing: so spent an uncomfortably cold night: IG officer with me.

3 December 1917

No breakfast: set out for Ytres & luckily found the Divisional train: had a nice breakfast with Lord Ailesbury,[34] & lunch: went on to Trescault to find GDA: ran them to ground at Neuville: had tea & dinner, & slept there.

4 December 1917

Went with Gen to Heudicourt & found 75th Brigade: went over to 'A' & remained until my fate may be decided.

5 December 1917

Very cold night & hard frost: walked over with Major to reconnoitre rear Positions in event of a recurrence of NOV 30th (Bosch counter attack on that day seems to have caught us napping: someone must be very much to blame: Gds saved situation.)[35] Colonel informed me I was to go as captain to 'C'.

6 December 1917

Went up with Major H to reconnoitre forward: still fine & frosty.

7 December 1917

Rather a heavy bombardment during the night: went over to 'C' Battery Gun Position & had lunch: severed connection for the time with 'A'. Rode down to the Waggon Line with Panton.[36] Frost came to an end: nasty cold muddy thaw.

8 December 1917

Rain in the night: mud again: heard that Gamble[37] had gone to a CCS: had dinner with Livingstone.[38]

Sunday 9 December 1917

Pouring with rain all night, & morning: wretched day: had tea with Padre.[39]

10 December 1917

Nice warm sunny day in contrast to preceding day. Changed horse lines. Tea at 'B' Bty.

11 December 1917

Cold Northerly wind got up during night: frost in morning. Brigade being relieved on nights of 12th–13th & 13th–14th. On 15th we march for 'somewhere'. Heard from Walter,[40] who was near Ypres: dined at 'B' Bty.

12 December 1917

Quite a nice day: men worked hard at harness & vehicles: Right Half Battery relieved & came to Waggon Line, & Tinkley.

13 December 1917

Rode up to Battery after breakfast, & heard that we march

out on 15th: remaining guns came down in evening: heard of capture of Jerusalem.[41]

14 December 1917

Nasty wet day: prepared for march on following day: went for ride with Seigne to Nurlu etc.

15 December 1917

Bde marched at 8.30 a.m.: via SOREL–FINS–EQUAN-COURT–YTRES Station-BUS (where we lunched & fed & watered horses)–ROCQUIGNY-LE TRANSLOY, to BEAU-LENCOURT, good camp on PERONNE road 1½ miles from BAPAUME.

16 December 1917

Left camp at 8.30 a.m. for HABARCQ (30 kils) via BAPAUME, Bihucourt, Courcelles, Ayette, BAUMETZ, Montenescourt: bad billets for officers, but men & horses good: snow set in after dark.

17 December 1917

2 inches of snow on the ground & hard frost: went looking for billets during the day: found a fairly comfortable Mess, & I managed to get a decent bedroom at the *Mairie*.[42]

The Colonel dined with us in the evening (a 5 course dinner!).

18 December 1917

Very hard frost & cold wind: otherwise a nice day: received my 6th parcel for Xmas. Major Hovil & Davies dined with us.

19 December 1917

Very hard frost again: in afternoon went with Seigne to track a wild pig, but failed to get up with it: Finch[43] & Banks dined with us.

20 December 1917

Left by motor bus at 9 a.m. with reps of each Bty (myself as OC 'A' Bty) to reconnoitre defence positions East of Arras near Athies. Lunched at Officers Club ARRAS: got back 4 p.m. Had dinner with 'A' Battery: Reid[44] joined Brigade.

The mairie *at Habarcq, where Eddie Giffard found a decent bedroom in December 1917.*

21 December 1917

Pig was killed at 2.30 p.m. Quiet day, otherwise.

22 December 1917

Attempted to thaw during middle of the day: rode into Duisans to get money, & met young Arnold-Forster.[45] Froze hard again in evening.

23 December 1917

Hard frost again: went into Avesnes in afternoon with Reid: dined at 'B' bty. Camp bed etc. arrived.

24 December 1917

Walked into DUISANS with 'John Willie'[46] to draw money: thaw set in a bit.

25 December 1917

Christmas Day! Men had a big dinner of Pork & Plum Pudding: we had our dinner in the evening: more snow: received letters from home. SEIGNE left for Course in England rather suddenly.

26 December 1917

Roads very slippery: had a concert in evening: borrowing 'B' Battery's piano: expect to leave for new waggon lines on January 1st.

27 December 1917

Roads still bad.

28 December 1917

All Sgts late on Parade! Very cold day: a little more snow fell in evening. Foley returned from leave.

29 December 1917

Quiet day: Foley & Williams came to tea.

Sunday 30 December 1917

Thawed a little: Football match in afternoon v 'A' Bty: scores one goal all.

31 December 1917

Hard frost again: expect to take over from 15th Division on 4th Jan, in the Line. Dined with 'B' Battery & went to their concert: but was disturbed in the middle of it, owing to a row in 'C': some of whom broke into an '*Estaminet*'.

1 January 1918

New Year's day: beautiful sunny morning: hard frost.

2 January 1918

Preparing for move: Rt Section move up on 3rd: taking over from C/71 15th Div.

3 January 1918

Left in Lorry at 9.45 a.m., for Bde HdQrs, which we reached at 11 a.m. (near FAMPOUX). Tinkley[47] and I stayed with C/71 for the night: fairly decent Position on the whole.

4 January 1918

Walked round with McCorquordale[48] to see advanced section, etc, & OP: remaining detachments came up at 5 p.m.

5 January 1918

Spent all the morning going through papers: went up to Bn HdQrs with Panton, & then on to OP in 'Corona' support near Roeux.

6 January 1918

Started work on forward section, on outskirts of FAMPOUX: went over to Brigade HeadQrs to tea. Thaw set in in evening.

7 January 1918

Raining slightly, and a fair thaw: walked up the Cam Valley with Major Hovil to reconnoitre alternative position. Remained in all the afternoon & evening going through defence scheme.

8 January 1918

Snowing, & a hard frost: visited Bn HdQrs (1st C Gds). Bitter cold wind in afternoon.

9 January 1918

Very hard frost: heard that I was detailed for BCs Course at Shoebury: Jan 20th. Walked with Emberton[49] to reconnoitre position for defence of Corps Line: snow blizzard in afternoon. Thawed again in evening.

10 January 1918

Very muddy: walked over to Brigade in morning with Wyatt:[50] saw an alternative position which, however, was not satisfactory.

11 January 1918

Went up to OP & Rt Co HdQrs, and battalion headquarters with Wyatt: got rather wet coming back. (7.30 a.m. went to reconnoitre alternative position, but this again was 'squashed'.)

12 January 1918

Walked over with Tinkley to alternative Position near 'B'/75 Position: this was approved of: at last!

13 January 1918

Vicinity of Battery shelled fairly heavily at intervals throughout the day. Went round front line, & visited Bn & rt Coy HdQrs: met Sutton-Nelthorpe.[51] No. 1 Gun Pit blown in.

14 January 1918

Went off early to register guns afresh, on a/c of rumours of short shooting: more snow again, but not cold: lunched at Bde HdQrs: thawed in evening.

15 January 1918

Warm, but horribly wet & windy later: went round to Bn HdQrs, & then on to alternative position: lunched with Foley. All dugouts leaking.

16 January 1918

Very wet & windy, & horrid: remained about Battery all day. Muscular rheumatism (?) during the night: Panton arrived at Bty Position to take over when I go.

17 January 1918

Horrid wet day again: went with Panton round forward section, Bde HdQrs, Alternative Position, & position for defence of 2nd system.

18 January 1918

Handed over all the papers to Panton & walked down with Emberton & lunched at ARRAS. Called at GDA for Tea & dined at Club. Left Arras at midnight & reached Boulogne at 8 a.m.

19 January 1918

Left Boulogne at 12 midday & arrived London 3.45 p.m., met by Dad & Maudie.

20 January–17 February 1918

Course at Shoebury and Salisbury.[52]

19 February 1918

Left Victoria at 7.50 a.m. & arrived Boulogne at 1.15 p.m.: remained there the night.

20 February 1918

Left at 11.57 a.m., & arrived ARRAS 6.15 p.m.: went up & dined at Club: slept at YMCA.

21 February 1918

Rode up to Bty, & walked round with Seigne: got back to Arras at 5.55 p.m. Dined at Officers Club with Hussey,[53] Davis [sic][54] and Stockton:[55] slept at YMCA.

22 February 1918

Rode up to Battery in morning, & got back to waggon line at 8 p.m., where I prepared to stay.

23 February 1918

Remained in waggon line: busy looking round.

24 February 1918

Rode up to 74th Bde HdQrs for 'Court of Enquiry'. Lunched at 'C' Bty position: & remained there till dark: got home to WL at 7.15 (about 7 miles).

25 February 1918

Horrible wet & windy day; lunched at Officers Club, with Godfrey:[56] & walk back to WL: heard that General had been round.

26 February 1918

Rather a nice sunny morning: remained at WL all day: Colonel Riddell went round in afternoon.

27 February 1918

Fine day: football match in afternoon: drew 1 all with 'A' Battery: had tea at GDA: turned into a wet night.

28 February 1918

Fine day: dug a site for 'E and Y' hut.[57]

1 March 1918

Cold day: rode up to Battery & remained there for lunch. Turned into horrid cold afternoon, with snow showers: got back at 5.10 p.m.: 'E and Y' hut erected. Great gale all night.

2 March 1918

Horrible cold day: snow set in after lunch: bitterly cold.

3 March 1918

Slightly warmer: turned to rain later: rode into Arras in evening for bath & dinner at Officers Club.

4 March 1918

6 a.m. heavy firing from direction of LENS: rode up to reconnoitre Reserve positions, had lunch at Battery. Panton received his Leave Warrant.

5 March 1918

Fine drying day: Panton proceeded on leave.

6 March 1918

Rather nice warm day: put horses outside: dined at Officers Club with JW.

7 March 1918

Nice sunny day again: managed to get the use of a very small rifle range: music in the evening.

8 March 1918

Lovely day: carried out Rifle practice with all the grooms & two grs: quite a success.

9 March 1918

Again a nice sunny day: rifle practice early. Clocks moved forward 1 hr at 11 p.m.

Sunday 10 March 1918

Nice sunny day again. Expected Bosch offensive did not materialize. Rode up to Battery after lunch.

11 March 1918

Rode up into Arras to draw money & paid out, at Waggon Line: Colonel Riddell came round in afternoon.

12 March 1918

Seigne rode down to Lunch & looked round Waggon Line: also Corps horsemaster.

13 March 1918

Still beautiful weather. Rode into Arras in afternoon to buy canteen stuff etc., & later walked in with 'John Willie' for a bath & dinner.

14 March 1918

A little rain at night, but fine day: rode into Arras calling at GDA.

15 March 1918

Fine sunny day, rather windy. Material was drawn for Horse standings: General came round the lines. Dined with JW.

16 March 1918

Another nice day: did some shopping in Arras: 'JW' dined with me.

17 March 1918

Woke up feeling rather 'queer' inside: went to bed early: Tinkley came down to Lunch & Wyatt in the evening to go on leave.

18 March 1918

Wyatt proceeded on leave. I felt better, but not quite right: Colonel Riddell came round lines in afternoon: heard that we change WLs about 21st.

19 March 1918

Very wet but warm; rain will probably do a lot of good. Officers of 135th Bty visited WL preparatory to taking over. Bathed & dined at club in evening with Davies.

20 March 1918

Wet morning, but fine later. Visited Waggon Line of 135th Bty[58] (Major Griffiths Williams): nice Horse lines & billets good too: right in Arras, near Station.

21 March 1918

Heavy bombardment at Dawn: Enemy HV Guns very active, St Pol even shelled. This was beginning of the Enemy offensive at last. Relief of GDA by 4th DA was changed, & the whole relief took place in evening, Waggon Lines exchanging in evening at 8.30 p.m. Arras shelled heavily throughout the day:[59] all settled in & went to bed at midnight.

22 March 1918

Went out reconnoitring Bty positions at 10.30 a.m., motor bussing through BEURAIN to NEUVILLE-VITASSE: walked about 10 miles: got back at 3.30 p.m. to find that Bde had just marched out to Positions at BEURAIN: (short lived rest). Enemy apparently have broken into our lines at CROISILLES, HENINEL & St LEGER: guns put in position & Waggon Lines formed near ACHICOURT at 8 p.m. At 10.30 orders to move guns received: harnessed up & moved guns & ammunition to Position just South of Mercatel. Refilled with amm, & got back to WL at 5.30 a.m.: watered & fed horses, also ourselves (23/3/918).

23 March 1918

(Continued) HV guns rather active round Arras & our WLs. Marched for new WLs near Blairville at 12.30 p.m., got in at 3 p.m. Went up with amm at 9.30 p.m., gun limbers also went up to move guns to new position S of BOISLEUX-au-MONT. Got back at 3 p.m. [*sic*], & had an awful job to load again owing to traffic congestion: sent waggons up again to Bty & slept myself from 5 a.m.–9 a.m.: two horses wounded, one had to be destroyed.

24 March 1918

Bosch appears to have got through down South: Peronne lost: had a good sleep.

25 March 1918

Rather a colder morning: we probably move waggon lines again. 5th Army has apparently been very roughly handled, & to be almost '*non est*' as a fighting force.[60] Moved battery in evening to a Waggon Line near Adinfer; rather a nasty journey up. Got in at 11 p.m. & spent a rather uncomfortable cold night in the open.

26 March 1918

Remained all morning in WL. At 1 p.m. moved out to take up position in the open: this was then cancelled,· & we returned & came into action near Waggon Line: & remained waiting for further orders.

27 March 1918

Got up at 1 a.m., & battery marched at 2.40 a.m. for new position at MOISZEAUX-A-MONT [?]: got into action at 4 a.m.: I took all waggons & salved remaining ammunition from former gun position. Bitterly cold. After breakfast moved WLs a little distance: & got Nissim [presumably Nissen] hut accommodation for whole waggon line.

12 midday: four bombs fell in camp, wounding fourteen of our horses: & 1 man: Ellis,[61] also wounded. 12.30 p.m. marched back to old WL, near Bretencourt [?]: two loads of amm sent up to guns: Bosch apparently attacking.

28 March 1918

12.30 a.m. 6 waggons of amm sent up, & another 6 at 5.30 p.m. Bitterly cold, but found cook's cart cover a fair shelter. Heard that Bosch were heavily attacking Divisions on our right & left (31st & 30th [?]). No more work during the day: heavy rain set in later: poured all night: & enjoyed a good night's sleep in Waddell's tent.

29 March 1918

Rain stopped, but very cold: heard that enemy had CORBIE: also that 4th Division had inflicted enormous losses on Hun in our old Positions North of the Scarpe.

30 March 1918

Cold, & wet later: Senior[62] & Panton[63] wounded: Foley went to command 'A': 74th WL shelled, & 20 casualties. Divisional WLs in consequence moved behind Bretencourt: very wet move & bad lines: found a billet in a house with Radford[64] & 'B' Bty. 12 waggons of amm sent up the line.

31 March 1918

Easter Sunday. Emberton turned uup from 'Le Touquet'. Changed WL to a decent spot: went up the line with Emberton and Henshaw:[65] lunched at Bty: found they had a piano: got back to WL at 5 p.m.: everything comfortably settled.

1 April 1918

Remained in Waggon Line: no fresh attack on our front. Nice spring day: Colonel wounded.[66]

2 April 1918

Attack by Huns expected, but did not take place: MacFadzean[67] dined with us.

3 April 1918

One gun moved for sniping purposes. Dined at Bde HdQrs & won 6 francs at Bridge. Moriarty and Mullen arrived[68] and joined battery.

4 April 1918

Moriarty went up to Bty: wet day: Read[69] came down & Wyatt returned from leave. Found two new billets for WL.

5 April 1918

Rode up to Bty with Mullen & found Seigne had been slightly wounded in cheek: Seigne went down for injection & I remained to command Bty. Having been heavily strafed in morning, moved Bty in evening further back. Uncomfortable night.

6 April 1918

Remained in Bty to settle down: rain set in in evening, & 4 of us spent uncomfortable night under tarpaulin: heard of Tinkley's death.

7 April 1918

Went up to forward OP in morning: Emberton departed for WL. Wyatt came up: very wet night.

8 April 1918

Wet morning: very difficult to get on with the work: improved our hut in the afternoon. Had tea at 'A' battery.

9 April 1918

Very foggy damp day: very muddy. Remained in battery: Seigne came up to lunch. WLs all parked together: as Brigade lines: nice mark for the Bosch.

10 April 1918

Dull foggy day: very little hostile activity: went up to forward OP, & registered forward gun: quiet night, warmer: heard that Bosch had captured Messines Ridge, & XIXth Div had recaptured it. Also that Bosch had broken through at Laventie.

11 April 1918

Went up to OP with Wyatt: rather nice day: called on Bn Commander.

12 April 1918

Beautiful sunny day: very good light: good deal of aerial activity. Major Corbett wounded slightly.

13 April 1918

Foggy day, rather colder: walked over to BLAIRVILLE with Foley: quiet day.

14 April 1918

Very cold windy day: visited forward gun(burial [?]), and reconnoitred routes. Had tea with 'A' Battery.

15 April 1918

Very cold day. Went up to forward OP, & registered guns: visited Bn HdQrs: Major Senior died of wounds.

16 April 1918

Attack on Left Bn: 'Assist Left' came into force: also counter preparation on SOS Lines. Went up later with Foley to forward OP & registered Bde SOS lines: much arty activity on the whole through the day & early night.

17 April 1918

Warmer day: walked up with Wyatt & visited Bn HdQrs (25th RF)[70] & on to OP: registered guns again & returned Bty to lunch. Rain set in, in afternoon. Seigne turned up to tea to take over Bty again: I returned to Waggon Line in evening.

18 April 1918

Wet day: Waggon Lines very muddy.

19 April 1918

Cold, & sleet showers: reconnoitred Bty positions at RANSART in morning. Campbell[71] joined Bde. Heard that Cropper[72] had died.

20 April 1918

Rather finer day: Gen Wilson visited lines. Reserve positions changed: reconnoitred them after tea. Heard that Col Rudkin was coming to command Bde.

21 April 1918

Cool fine day: Maj Housden[73] visited the waggon lines: Church parade: went for a ride with Radford in afternoon. Emberton went up the Line.

22 April 1918

Nothing but rumours of changing position.

23 April 1918

Rode up to the Battery for Lunch: nice warm day. Dined with 'A' Bty: much artillery activity during the night.

24 April 1918

Dull foggy day. Housden, Davis lunched with us. Went for a ride with Wyatt after tea.

25 April 1918

Warm day, but showery. Heard of raid on Zeebrugge, & of new Colonel's arrival. Rode with Radford round Berles-au-Bois, Pommier, La Cauchie etc.

26 April 1918

Col Rudkin[74] inspected Waggon Lines: & remained for night: rumours of moving batteries & WLs.

27 April 1918

Rode over to see prospective WLs at Gaudiempre (32nd DA) got back at 2.30 p.m.

28 April 1918

Rode up with Radford to see new Bty position & forward WLs: prepared to march on 29th.

29 April 1918

Marched out at 10.30 a.m.: & reached new WLs at 1.15 p.m.: 168 Bde took over our lines, & we certainly got the worst of the exchange.

30 April 1918

Horrible wet day: rode up to forward WL & Bty position: got back at 4 p.m.

1 May 1918

Very cold & drizzling morning: remained in W-Lines: dined with Bird.[75]

2 May 1918

A nice sunny summer day at last! General visited lines: genial as ever. Rode into HUMBERCAMPS in afternoon, & back by St AMAND: Wyatt went up to the guns: I had notice to come up on 3rd.

3 May 1918

Rode up to guns at 10 a.m.: took over from Major, who proceeded to WL for a week: went up to rear OP & night OP: quite close to Bty.

4 May 1918

Went with Foley to Bn HdQrs 1st I Gds, & back via Forward gun (anti-tank [?] where Emberton was in charge):

met Major Corbett at 'B' battery, just returned from Hospital.

5 May 1918

Got up at 4.30 a.m., & went with Foley & Wyatt to the forward OP: in a sap: very foggy & could see nothing: reconnoitred Purple line positions in afternoon & had tea at Bde.

At 10.30 p.m. heard that Corbett had been sniped dead in front line: great loss to Brigade.

6 May 1918

Walked over to Bde with Foley in morning: & looked at Purple positions in afternoon: & forward WL. Very wet night, & most Dugouts flooded.

7 May 1918

Walked down to forward gun in morning, and to FWL & reserve positions in afternoon. Moriarty came up to Bty in evening: much 'wind' up over 'expected' Bosh attack.

8 May 1918

Warm muggy day, but fine: went with Foley to Bn HdQrs of 2 G Gds & 1st I Gds in morning. Walked over with Emberton to FWL in evening.

9 May 1918

Fine hot day again: went forward & registered Bty on Zero Lines: Foley went over to command 'B' & Holt[76] to 'A'.

10 May 1918

Walked down to Antitank gun & Bns HdQrs in morning. Major came up after tea, & I rode down to Waggon Line.

11 May 1918

Remained in W Lines.

12 May 1918

Cold day: & more rain. Had dinner at HdQ WL.

13 May 1918

31 years of age!
    Horrible wet day: General visited lines.

14 May 1918

Fine day: rode into Humbercamps to get money for pay. 5 parcels arrived: dined with J.W. at 'B' Bty WL.

15 May 1918

Nice hot day again. Two HV shell fell near GAUDIEMPRE. Rode out in afternoon to see 'Red' line positions: much aeroplane activity throughout the day.

16 May 1918

Hot day: rode up the line with the Doctor:[77] had tea at Battery: big Bosch attack apparently expected.

17 May 1918

Another hot day: Mullen went up the line, & Emberton came down.

18 May 1918

Hot day, but thunder-shower in afternoon: as there were many planes about during night, we started bomb-proofing huts & horse lines.

19 May 1918

Whitsunday. Lovely day again: service in the open for the Div Arty. Dined with Henshaw & Waddell. General visited lines.

20 May 1918

Another lovely day with cool breeze: a few HV shell fell on Southern portion of GAUDIEMPRE. Went for a ride with Emberton: tea'd at 'A' Battery. Henshaw[78] & Waddell dined with us: heard that Foley[79] had been wounded. Very hard luck on him! Much wind, up the line; Bosch expected to attack.

[The fourth notebook concludes with map references of gun positions, etc., and with the following memorandum:]

22 August 1917

Wager with major.

XIVth Corps	2000 prisoners	@ 1 centime
	15 guns	@ 50 centimes

7

Eddie's Diary: The Fifth Notebook

E. H. Giffard C/75 RFA

21 May 1918

Rode into Humbercamps for money: nice day again.[1] Colonel came down to Gaudiempre for a week's rest.

22 May 1918

Another lovely day. Colonel came round the lines: Seigne came down to WL: & Emberton[2] went up to Gun Position for the day: Emberton returned at Midnight.

23 May 1918

Emberton went up to stay at Gun Position: very strong wind during day. A new Major[3] posted to 'B'; so my own chances again 'knocked on the head'.

24 May 1918

Got wet through taking early exercise: heavy rain: General visited the lines. Dined at Bde HdQrs in the evening.

25 May 1918

Fine again. Rode to the new Red Line positions in afternoon with Finch.[4] POMMIER. Had tea with Hancock[5] & dined with Henshaw.[6]

26 May 1918
Fine day after foggy morning. Remained in W Lines all day. Henshaw dined with me.

27 May 1918
General visited lines again: Bde sports in afternoon. Saulty railhead intermittently shelled throughout day by HV gun (9.4"?).

28 May 1918
Took early exercise: Wyatt[7] came down for the afternoon: rode back as far as Pommier with him & dined at Bde WL HdQrs: news of German attack on the Aisne does not seem too promising.

29 May 1918
Gen Fielding inspected Wagon Lines in morning. Rode into PAS with Radford[8] & Finch[9] in afternoon, & made a few purchases. A good deal of bombing during the night.

30 May 1918
Rode up to Bty at 9.30 a.m. to take over from Major for a few days.

31 May 1918
Lovely day again. News from the AISNE front appeared very bad: MARNE crossed by the Germans.

1 June 1918
Went to Ironside post and Rook's Nest OPs, & remained in Bty for rest of day: Hun Arty fairly active in evening: & up to midnight .

2 June 1918
2 a.m.–3 a.m. quite a heavy gas 'strafe': which necessitated

helmets being worn for a short while. Went out at 5 a.m. & visited Bn HdQrs & anti-tank gun: found Wyatt in bed. Walked down to FWL after Breakfast.

3 June 1918

Went down to FWL in morning: Hun vigorously shelled an empty position, most of the day.

4 June 1918

HdQrs 75th Bde went out: we come under Colonel Vickery[10] & go into Left Group: visited forward WL, & walked in evening to New Bde OP in Adinfer Wood: later registered guns afresh on Aerodrome.

5 June 1918

Got up at 3.30 a.m., & went with Wyatt to Adinfer Wood OP, thence on by myself to Bn HdQrs & Antitank gun:[11] got back at 6.30 & had a bath. Heavy shells (8") were put over towards RANSART during morning.

6 June 1918

Went out with Holt,[12] to forward posts to fire on new SOS Lines: returned via forward anti-tank gun & Adinfer Wood OP: very quiet day.

7 June 1918

Rode down to Wagon Line at 9 a.m. General Wilson,[13] Col., Corps Horsemaster, & BGRA all came round the lines: rode back after tea.

8 June 1918

Went round with Emberton to Bn HdQrs (24th RFs[14] IInd Div): anti-tank gun & Adinfer Wood OP: found that Bde positions had been harassed with 8" during our absence.

9 June 1918

'A' Bty intermittently crumped with 5.9" & 8" during the day. Walked out to reconnoitre the Bde positions in X 2 & 3 in afternoon: quiet night.

10 June 1918

Rode down at 7 a.m. to WL. A little rain fell: barely enough to lay the dust: preparing to move out on the 12th: rode back to Battery at 5.30 p.m.

11 June 1918

Heard that we do not move till the 14th & 15th: CRA of 40th DA visited the Bty: checked zero lines. Walked down to FWL in afternoon, & to X 2 & 3 positions after tea with Emberton.

12 June 1918

Walked up to Adinfer Wood OP, & then with Wyatt to forward gun, & Company HdQrs: called in at Bn HdQrs, on way back: 5.9" fell about 300x to Rt flank of Bty from 12.30 p.m. to 3 p.m.: 8" then fell near 'D' bty: harassing fire.

13 June 1918

10 a.m. violent attack of toothache! 2 darts of Brandy. Very quiet day: usual walk to FWL. Emberton went up to relieve Wyatt at OP. Move into rest cancelled.

14 June 1918

Went up to OP and then with Emberton to post 5: Coy HdQrs, & forward gun: got back to Bty at 3.15 p.m.

15 June 1918

75th Bde came into action from 6 a.m.: saw Major Dresser.

16 June 1918
Rode down to Wagon Line at 9.30 a.m.: & returned to tea at HdQrs at 4.30 p.m.: when scheme for raid was discussed.

17 June 1918
9.30 a.m. to 10.30 a.m. another violent attack of toothache: General Wilson visited batteries during morning: walked down to Bde in morning: quiet day.
   Barrage for raid opened at 11.35 p.m.: stood to till 1.30 a.m.

18 June 1918
Walked down to Bn HdQrs & forward gun: back via Adinfer Wood OP. FWL & Bde in afternoon. Saw announcement of Major's engagement.

19 June 1918
Rain during the night & a wet morning. Walked down to RANSART dressing station, & went on to BAC-de-SUD to try & get dental treatment, & failed & returned walking from BEAUMETZ: quiet day.

20 June 1918
Went down to forward gun, & back via Adinfer Wood OP: quiet day.

21 June 1918
Left at 7.15 a.m. to ride to BAC-de-SUD: got an Ambulance from there to FREVENT. Had my tooth successfully extracted: got back to RANSART at 4.15 p.m. by Ambulance to SAULTY & thence Lorry-jumping. The Major returned.

22 June 1918
Walked out with Holt to see new Purple Line positions near

BERLES. Emberton went down to Wagon Line. In afternoon visited Bn HdQrs, Anti-tank gun, and Adinfer Wood OP: very windy day.

23 June 1918

Remained in Bty: the Major turned up at Lunch time. Rode down & joined Emberton at W Line in evening.

24 June 1918

Rode out with Radford to COUTERELLE [*sic*] to see NCOs' & men's jumping: Sergeant McGregor 3rd. Turned into wet afternoon. Radford dined with us.

25 June 1918

Wet & windy: dined at Bde HdQrs.

26 June 1918

Half holiday: played 'A' Bty at cricket: beaten by 24 runs. Tea with Henshaw.

27 June 1918

Went out with early exercise: lovely day: in afternoon rode over to LUCHEUX with Emberton. Henshaw dined with us: we then went to 'B' Bty for the gramophone.

28 June 1918

Rode into BAVINCOURT with Emberton to IOM: quiet day.

29 June 1918

Went out with early exercise, & left for gun position at 9 a.m.: remained there for the day. Gen Wilson visited gun position, with Major York[15] the new BMRA. Got back at 11 p.m.

Sunday 30 June

Fine hot day. Went for a ride in the afternoon: played cricket in the evening: Finch dined with us.

1 July 1918

Hot day: went to see the preliminary trial 'Section' turn-out in afternoon at Couturelle. D/75 placed first.

2 July 1918

Left at 8.15 a.m. for Bty position to spend day: Major went down to attend lst Gds Bde Gymkhana. Got back to WL at 11 p.m.

3 July 1918

Half holiday cricket match in afternoon: beat 'B' Bty WL.

4 July 1918

Tried to find Red Line position for 3rd time, but failed to find board: nice hot day again: rode into 'Pas' in evening with Read & made some purchases.

5 July 1918

Dull day but fine: cricket practice in evening. Dined at HdQrs WL.

6 July 1918

Hot day: drew money for pay from HUMBERCAMP: paid out in evening.

7 July 1918

Hot day: felt a little 'fluey': beat 'D' Bty at cricket in the afternoon. Dined with Henshaw. Colonel returned from leave.

8 July 1918

Another warm day: Colonel visited lines: approved of horses but not of vehicles.

9 July 1918

A wet day: rumours of going out but nothing definite.

10 July 1918

Showery day: Corps horse & transport show near COUTURELLE: went over to see it in afternoon: D/75 did not manage to pull the section prize off. Walked to BAZEQUE Wood with Doctor to buy WSCE.[16]

11 July 1918

Showery day: took early exercise: Colonel visited lines, & expressed satisfaction: BSM interviewed, with a view to his 'going'.

12 July 1918

Horrible wet morning: Read[17] 'enjoyed' early exercise. Heard that my Leave Warrant had been applied for!! Cleared up in afternoon.

13 July 1918

Took early exercise & rode up to Bty to lunch: reconnoitred the BERLES-au-BOIS Wagon lines, & got back at 5.15 p.m.: played Bridge at Bde after dinner.

Sunday 14 July 1918

Turned into a wet day & cleared up at 5 p.m.: rode up with Read to BERLES, where he remained with a working party.

15 July 1918

Very hot muggy day: made preparations for moving the WLs the next day: dined at Bde HdQrs.

16 July 1918

Heavy thundershower at 6 a.m. till 7.30 a.m.: moved out of WLs at 10.15 a.m.: reached BERLES at 1 p.m.: remaining 4 guns came down in evening: no accommodation except what we carried: we would have been more comfortable remaining in action.

17 July 1918

Very hot day again: getting lines straightened up. Rode down to Bazeque Wood with Emberton in afternoon: received Leave Warrant at 5 p.m.: this was cancelled at 9 p.m.

18 July 1918

Hot day & thunder showers: Colonel went round the lines.

19 July 1918

Cooler day: great news of the French advance.[18] General visited the lines.

20 July 1918

Rode into Humbercamp to get money to pay with: paid out in evening. Dined at 'A'.

Sunday 21 July 1918

'B' bty beat 'D' at cricket. Went & had dinner at 'GOUY' with Moriarty[19] at No. 12 Balloon Co. Got back at 11.30 p.m.: much nocturnal aerial activity.

22 July 1918

Fine day: rode up to Ransart in morning to look for grass, & material. Played cricket in evening.

23 July 1918

Usual routine. Camp shelled at midnight by light HV gun: had to turn out & move horses.

24 July 1918

Fine day: Bosch HV guns a little more active: played 'A' Bty at cricket in the evening: beat them by 116 runs to 38: made 30 myself.

25 July 1918

The Major, Emberton & Wyatt left with all guns in the early morning to go to Occoches, 19 miles: to calibrate.

5.20 a.m. aroused by shells passing overhead: left X had a near shave. Showers all day. HdQrs beat 'B' at cricket.

26 July 1918

Showery day again: took Bty staff out in afternoon. Guns arrived back at 10 p.m.: very wet night: tent leaking badly.

27 July 1918

Wet morning; lines in an awful mess. Cleared up towards evening. Dined with the Colonel[20] at 'A' Bty.

28 July 1918

Fine day. Church parade in morning: final of Bde cricket tournament began at 1.30 p.m. 'C' Bty beat HdQrs by 12 runs, in a double innings match: got a bruise on the forehead: Colonel disabled.

29 July 1918

Fine & warm again: Bde sports in afternoon & G Gds Band. JW to dinner in evening.

30 July 1918

Another warm day. Took Bty staff out in afternoon. 'Inside' rather upset: poisoned probably.

31 July 1918

Not feeling very fit inside: a good party from Bde went to Gymkhana at BAZEQUE.

1 August 1918

Fine hot day: went for Drill Order in morning: informed that I go on leave on August 6th: a few shell fell in the village during the evening: Henshaw dined with us.

2 August 1918

Shifted down to a new Mess, under a roof: rather comfortable for a change: wet day. General Fielding visited lines in evening. Received leave warrant.

3 August 1918

Wet showery day: rode to Humbercamp for money: preparing for mounted sports. Dined at 'B' Bty: a few shell fell near lines at 11.15 p.m.

4 August 1918

Fine day: heard of fresh Allied successes: Soissons, etc. Church parade in morning. Preparing for mounted sports.

5 August 1918

Rode into Saulty & travelled down to Boulogne with Stephenson & Dawson:[21] getting in at 9 p.m.: 7 hrs from Doullens. Stopped at Hotel Folkestone.

6 August 1918

Crossed over at 3 p.m.: rather rough & felt 'squirmy'. Reach Folkestone 4.45 p.m., Victoria 7.40 p.m.: dined at Arty M Hotel with Maudie.

20 August 1918

Left Victoria at 7.50 a.m.: seen off by Dad, Polly, Maud[22] &

Bobbie:[23] spent 4 hours at Folkestone: reach Boulogne at 4.30 p.m. Met Hay,[24] & stayed at Folkestone Hotel for night.

21 August 1918

Left Boulogne at 11.47 a.m. & reached Saulty with a splitting headache at 9.15 p.m.: stopped at rest camp for the night.

22 August 1918

Made my way to GDA & found out that VIth Corps had advanced a bit, & Moyenville [sic] taken: went to rear WL at Bailleulmont, & found that most of wagon line had gone to position between Blaireville [sic] & Ransart (Major Dresser wounded slightly). Found FWL, & went on to Bde for tea: returned to WL at 7 p.m. and took over from Gascoigne-Cecil:[25] advance apparently beginning on most of 3rd Army front.

23 August 1918

Heavy bombardment began on our front at dawn: also further South: rode up to Bde & Bty, & found that all objectives had been taken, & bosch not showing much opposition: Heavy bombardment down South at 11 a.m.: lunch at Bde: all Bties probably move forward during the night.

24 August 1918

Moved limbers & amm wagons to Bty position BOIRY-St Martin at 1 p.m., & then took guns & amm up to position behind JUDAS Farm; & wagon lines to Boiry sugar factory: Water a difficult question: sent up more amm during the night: St Leger, Croisilles & MORY in our hands.

25 August 1918

Moved firing Bty[26] up to position near HAMELINCOURT,

& awaited all the morning for orders to move guns forward: went over later & had lunch at the guns, & met the new Colonel, Kirkland[27] by name: took limbers & wagons back at 6 p.m.: great clouds of dust about.

26 August 1918

Heavy rain during the night: Reveille 4 a.m.: Read took Firing Bty up to a position near guns: rode up myself later & reconnoitred new W Lines: good news of advance on left & capture of MONCHY-le-PREUX, by Canadians, & advance beyond Hindenburg line.

27 August 1918

Took Fng Bty up to position near battery (Reveille 3.30 a.m.). Attack commenced on our front at 7 a.m.: about 9.15 a.m. Left X went forward under Emberton & remainder of Bty followed later: found that enemy were nearer than expected & Left X were machine-gunned as they went over the crest: narrow shave: finally got a position further back, after an exciting day: 'B' Battery less fortunate: 'Cecil'[28] killed & J. Williams[29] wounded: moved W Lines up a bit further.

28 August 1918

Reveille 5.15 a.m.: took up firing Bty & Wagons to position of assembly: & waited till 5 p.m., when we moved up to Bty position, but were sent back almost directly: Capt Cecil buried.

29 August 1918

A peaceful night, & a good sleep, undisturbed. 2 p.m. the expected message arrived to send up gun limbers etc: we waited from 3.30 p.m. to 9.30 p.m. & then were sent back.

30 August 1918

Left about 7.30 a.m. with Firing battery & halted in rear of position: attack supposed to have gone well. Moved guns forward later about 2,000x, also W Lines. Met Godfrey[30] in the evening and dined with him.

31 August 1918

Rode up to Bty position after Breakfast & lunched there: Colonel visited Wagon Lines in afternoon. Water question still bad.

1 September 1918

Took Firing Bty etc up to position at 10 p.m., & move guns on to new position near Vraucourt [Vaulx-Vraucourt?]: much Hun bombing: got back at 2 a.m.: Howfield ('B' Bty) killed in the morning:[31] & buried at Hamelincourt.

2 September 1918

Went up with 'outfit' again at 10 a.m., & stood ready to move guns: went home at 4 p.m.: Wyatt rode down with me.

3 September 1918

Reveille 4.30 a.m. & move up to position by 7.00 a m. Heard that Boche had gone right back: move guns to position well East of Lagnicourt: moved up wagon lines to B17D (old Bty position): water question[32] very acute: got back at 10 p.m.

4 September 1918

Reveille 3.30 a.m.: to move up all waggons to position, near Battery: remained there till 6.45 p.m., & then went home (having wasted another day).

5 September 1918

Left undisturbed in the morning: rode over to GOMIE-COURT in afternoon, & drew money from Officers Club; also enjoyed a lemon squash: got back at 5.45 p.m. & found that wagon lines were just starting to move to new Lines North of Lagnicourt, & near QUEANT: most uncomfortable getting in in the dark: shelling unpleasantly near during the night.

6 September 1918

Watered early in QUEANT: & took nearly 2 hrs about it. Very hot day: rode up to Bty after breakfast, to find out orders. Found out that we move guns forward about 2 miles, after dusk. Got up to Bty with teams at 8.15 p.m.: & set off on our journey. Quiet at first, but later hun guns got very active, giving us an exciting time, especially on return journey: Bombs as well. Got back to W Lines at 2.30 a.m., only to find that Wagon Lines area was being shelled. Queant is a decidedly unhealthy spot.

7 September 1918

Not much sleep: moved W Lines back to near VRAU-COURT: very warm day: found some accommodation in Prisoners of War Cage.

6.30 p.m. got a sudden message to move guns from forward position back further: took Gun limbers up, & all went off alright: got back into bed at 3 a.m.

8 September 1918

Change in the weather: S.Wly wind & rain: quiet day: only a little Ammunition to shift: everyone at last have had a little rest: Emberton came down to W Line, preparatory to going on leave. Broad gauge railway already beyond VRAUCOURT.

9 September 1918

Showery day: paid out Wagon Line. Visited Officers Club at VRAUCOURT.

10 September 1918

Weather still showery: Lunched at Officers Club with Emberton, Doctor & Henshaw. No fighting locally.

11 September 1918

Feeling a bit seedy when I woke up: Emberton went off on leave: Wyatt came down to Lunch: small attack in the evening. Dined with Downing,[33] & felt very seedy when I went to bed. 11 p.m. message from Major that he was slightly wounded, & asking me to come up: too ill to do so. Read also slightly wounded.[34]

12 September 1918

Heard that Patterson[35] of 'B' had been badly wounded. Attack in the morning supposed to be successful. Havrincourt village taken. Remained in bed all day: saw the Major in the afternoon.

13 September 1918

Still remained in bed: no appetite: not feeling up to much. Phipps,[36] the new AVC officer arrived: heard that Americans had successfully attacked at St Michiel: 8,000 prisoners.

14 September 1918

Got up after breakfast: felt a little better: still showery weather. Heard that Napier[37] was missing: no trace of him. American success apparently increasing.

15 September 1918

A decent fine day at last: information that guns would probably be moved forward in the evening: this afterwards cancelled. Napier's body was found in trench forward: buried at LAGNICOURT. American success apparently complete.

16 September 1918

Fine day. Rode up to Bty & saw new position, near 'A' Bty. Lunched at Bty & got back to tea: sent up limbers & Amm wagons to move 2 guns to new position. Great thunderstorm during the night.

17 September 1918

Remained in Wagon Line till 5.30 p.m., when I took up 3 limbers & 6 amm wagons to move remainder of guns forward: this was cancelled on arrival at Bty position: & so I dined at Bty & got back at 10 p.m.: a good sleep.

18 September 1918

Heavy rain during early morning. Rode up to Bty at 11 a.m., to relieve Major for a few days. Walked with him to forward X OP & Bde HdQrs: heavy enemy bombardment broke out at 4 p.m.: apparently an attack on HAVRIN-COURT: had to wear gas helmets for a time. Got back to rear position at 7 p.m.: major rode down to WLs.

19 September 1918

Walked over to forward X to stay: checked lines in afternoon.

20 September 1918

Attended BCs' Conference: Bties to be moved up to forward positions on Y/Z night (about 25th). Reconnoitred position near Demicourt: 1,000 rds amm sent up there in evening. Wire cutting also has to be carried out.

21 September 1918

Took Lindsey[38] up to new position: & then went on to APE OP to cut wire: communication bad but managed to fire later in the evening. Heavy Bosch barrage on MOEVRES during afternoon, & Bty areas.

22 September 1918

Remained in Bty most of the day: visited Bde later on in evening: 'B' Bty pulled remaining X out. Holt[39] went off to Hospital, & leave.

23 September 1918

Showery morning: went down with Henshaw to new forward position: no news of Z day. Heard extraordinary success in Palestine.[40] Had tea at Bde. A very nasty night: no sleep: 15 Gn Hows active round position all night.

24 September 1918

Remained in Bty all day. Major reconnoitred canal crossings.[41] Quiet night.

25 September 1918

Went down with Wyatt to new positions, & marked out lines of fire, & got amm straight.

At 8.15 p.m. took 2 forward X guns in, and met Read with the other 4 at new position. One horse wounded. Z day probably 27th.

26 September 1918

Went over to rear position to meet Major at 10 a.m. He took over the Bty again: rather to my sorrow. I went back to Wagon Line in afternoon, & made ready to move whole W Line at Dawn: Zero Hour 5.20 a.m.: as usual there were usual vague rumours as to extent of attack.

27 September 1918

5.20 a.m. Bombardment broke out: moved wagon lines to old Bty position (J2 B), & met the Major later near Demicourt. Moved guns forward via Hermies & canal to position West of Flesquieres: very little hostile shelling.

Shifted guns a little further forward at 8 p.m.: got back to W Lines at HERMIES at 1.30 a.m.

28 September 1918

Firing Bty ordered up at 10 a.m.: rather wet: moved guns forward to Orival Wood in afternoon: very little Bosch Arty activity. Cambrai appears not to be held by enemy: got back to Wagon Line at 7 p.m.

29 September 1918

Reveille 4.45 am: took Firing Bty up to guns & found new Wagon Line near FLESQUIERES. CAMBRAI appears to have fallen. Our Infantry have crossed the Canal D'ESCAUT. 2.30 p.m. Firing Bty odered up to move guns forward: to near 'Nine Wood': got back to wagon lines after the usual trouble over watering, at 8.30 p.m. in pouring rain: Emberton got back in afternoon.

30 September 1918

Firing Bty went up to guns & whole wagon line ordered up: but afterwards cancelled. Camped for night at quarry near Nine Wood & with the limbers & wagons: about 4,000x from Bosch.

1 October 1918

Remainder of wagon line got up at Midday: one horse fatally wounded during night, & 'Gipsy' and S-M's horse wounded in afternoon: decided to move Wagon Lines to healthier situation & nearer Bty. Firing Bty camped for night in new W Lines.

2 October 1918

Moved remainder of W Line to new position near Bty & comfortably situated as to accommodation.

3 October 1918

Watered at river in front of guns! Unexpected message at Midday to move W Lines back to Quarry near last one: very annoyed about it just as we were getting settled in. Moved over after lunch & got cover myself (& Lindsay) with 'A' Bty for night. Heard of capture of St Quentin, Aubers Ridge & Damascus.

4 October 1918

Fine day, & breakfasted in open: decided to mess with 'A' Battery. General visited lines: rather a nasty night with 77 mms falling in close proximity to horses. Turkey[42] out of it.

5 October 1918

Orders to move to Doignies, out with guns, afterwards cancelled: guns only coming out for Mobile Reserve into present Wagon Lines. Reconnoitred new wagon lines a little further back, with the Major. Rt X went over there in the evening, with Lindsay.

6 October 1918

Orders to reconnoitre new positions near Rumilly, & to take guns in, in the evening: for attack next morning. This was postponed 24 hrs, so we all remained at W Lines.

7 October 1918

Made preparations for moving guns into new forward positions: took some Amm up in afternoon & dumped it as near position as possible. Refilled & took Amm up in the dark: Amm & guns got in without accident: last teams got back about 11 p.m.

8 October 1918

Attack at 4.30 a.m. in the morning [*sic*]: sent up 600 rds of Ammunition: C sub Gun team 'wiped out', by stray shell: Cpl

Hall, & two Dvrs[43] killed, & 1 wounded: very hard luck. German tanks caused a surprise in the morning, but were effectively dealt with, & attack in afternoon reach final objectives: many prisoners came in. Firing Bty, & wagons went up with view to moving guns, but were sent back. Got back at midnight: bad blocks on the road.

9 October 1918

Up early: Reveille 4 a.m.: moved guns forward to near WAMBAIX, & Wagon lines to LESDAIN, where we occupied the Chateau for the night.[44] Villages now show some signs of civilization: an advance of 5 or 6 miles. Heard that I was given A/75.

10 October 1918

Reveille 5 a.m.: moved up to gun position, & took guns to position East of BOUSSIERES. Wagon Lines moved to ESTORMEL. Took over 'A' Bty from Henshaw in the evening: got comfortable dugouts for the night.

11 October 1918

Moved guns forward to position just S of St Hillaire [*sic*]: raining all day: went up to observe a shoot from the Presbytery, St Hillaire [*sic* again], & Bosch seemed to rather object to it: had a good sleep under the Gun cover: Grantham[45] joined us, from the Shop:[46] Reid returned to 'C'.

12 October 1918

Orders to move guns forward cancelled. FOOs sent out from Bties. Battery moved at Midday to position between QUIEVY & Viesly: pouring wet night: remained there without firing a round; Hall went on leave.

13 October 1918

Moved Bty at 06.30 hours to position near La Torte Farm:[47]

just got teams away when 15 CN searched position, Grantham wounded badly in hand, & less severely in knee: myself slight one in left arm. Dartnall[48] having gone forward, I was left without another officer. Bosch rather nasty all day:

The farm at Fontaine-au-Tertre, where Eddie's battery was in action in 1918.

Emberton took over from me 5 p.m. I walked to ADS, St Hillaire: thence to MDS,[49] CARNIERES, where OC 3rd FA put me up for night: enjoyed a good meal & sleep.

Anti-tetanus injection rather irritating.

14 October 1918

Left at 11 a.m. for 29th CCS BEUGNY: met Bird[50] there, & found there was nothing in my arm, but very swollen. Had a good sleep.

15 October 1918

Dull rainy day: heard in the afternoon that we were to go to 'Grevillers'. Arrived at 49th CCS at 6.45 p.m. Enjoyed my dinner (beer & Port), a very comfortable place, & nice people.

Had a sound sleep.
Splendid news of Flanders offensive.

16 October 1918
Stayed in bed to breakfast: arm still rather swollen. Got up after breakfast & enjoyed an easy day.

17 October 1918
Breakfast in bed: walked to Achiet-le-Grand in afternoon, & found on return that Hughes[51] had arrived at No. 34 CCS (across the road) suffering from old gas burns: went over to see him.

18 October 1918
Swelling in arm quite down, & wound healing. Prepared to leave with Bird after lunch, to rejoin. Picked up a motor as far as SERANVILLERS, thence got to St Hillaire at 20.00, (75th HdQrs), dined there & slept the night.
OSTEND, LILLE, BRUGES etc Captured.

19 October 1918
Went to Wagon Line after breakfast, at Quievy, saw Stockton,[52] & got up to Bty to lunch & took over from Emberton: went up to OP in afternoon, & thence walked to Bde HQ for BCs' conference: attack 0200 hrs on the morrow.
Spent remainder of night up, working out Barrage etc.

20 October 1918
1 a.m. Dartnall[53] went off to OP: 2 a.m. attack commenced. Poured with rain: at 6.15 a.m. went out with other BCs to reconnoitre. Nasty Barrage along railway. Made another reconnaissance in afternoon; across the Stelle [*sic*] remained in old position for night, & all enjoyed a good sleep.

21 October 1918

Orders at 9.15 a.m. to move forward Guns across the river Selle: reconnnitred route via HAUSSY: got into action at 3 p.m.: GS wagon with the rations on broke down, & did not arrive till after dark. Rain fortunately kept off till we had got under cover.

22 October 1918

Reconnoitred an OP with Darley[54] before breakfast: rain set in again after breakfast. General Wilson visited Bties. Barrage Map for attack came in 9 p.m., & so had plenty to do.

23 October 1918

Attack began at 3.20 a.m. Hun did a lot of shelling all through the night, & some near ones round Bty: Holloway[55] rather badly wounded in arm, & had to go to Hospital: Sgt Tetley[56] also wounded. After being in doubt as to whether we moved, we got orders at 4 p.m. to move across the HAPIES via VERTAIN: got guns into position at 1 p.m.: attack quite successful. Got into bed at 1 p.m. [*sic*, presumably a.m.]

24 October 1918

Attack renewed at 4 a.m.: again completely successful. Orders to move back to W Lines at HAUSSY at 4 p.m.: guns left under a guard in case of enemy counter-attack.

Got down to HAUSSY at 7 p.m., & found Waddell had got us nice billets near the church: enjoyed civilization once more.

25 October 1918

Busy looking round the lines etc: General visited lines, & picked out debility cases.

26 October 1918

Nice fine day: withdrew guns to W Line: rode to VERTAIN in afternoon.

27 October 1918

Sudden orders to move to Wagon Lines at St HILLAIRE: got there at 4 p.m.: fairly decent billets.

28 October 1918

Cleaning up all over again: billets, harness, wagons etc.

29 October 1918

The same.

30 October 1918

Colonel inspected us in Marching Order: dined with 'B' battery.

31 October 1918

Colder day: lecture in evening to Bde by Rev H. W. Head.[57]

1 November 1918

Definite orders that we move into action on following day: to support big attack. All inspections off: my arm decidedly better.

2 November 1918

We left St Hilaire at 9 a.m. for wagon lines near BERMERAIN. Went on ahead with small staff (via St Python, Vertain, Escarmain & Capelle), & met Colonel with other BCs at 11.00. Chose position for Bty, & went back to wagon lines: pouring with rain all day. Felt very seedy, & so took Hall up to position: & left Waddell to bring up guns, & take command for night.

3 November 1918

Still feeling bad so left Waddell to do the Barrage.

4 November 1918

Wagon Lines left soon after 7 a.m.: for Bty position & the

'Blue': went up with guns through VILLERS-POL,[58] & saw Waddell, & then went back & established Wagon lines in VILLERS-POL. Feeling rather 'seedy'. Got into a drafty cottage for the night: a wretched night with griping pains: attack, on wide front, appears to have gone wall.

5 November 1918

Reveille 4 a.m.: sent Abley[59] off with the Wagon Lines, & remained with Kane[60] in Villers-Pol to try & recuperate. Left at 3 p.m. to try & find Bty: after a tiring journey through FRASNOY & Gommegnies, to outskirts of AMFROIPRET, found them at 6.45 p.m.

6 November 1918

Rather an uncomfortable night from point of view of 'tummy', & Bosch shelling: Wagon lines were moved up at 9.30 a.m. & moved back again at Midday, as Bosch had not apparently cleared out as far as expected: 5 horses and 3 Dvrs wounded.[61]
   Quiet night: good rest.

7 November 1918

Advance continued. Took over from Waddell[62] east of MECQUIGNIES, & liaised with Bn. Finally put section in action at MALGARNI: quiet up till 3.30 p.m.: from then till 7 p.m. most 'unhealthy': W Lines at MECQUIGNIES. Quiet night & good rest after all.

8 November 1918

All sorts of rumours of Armistice: Bosch deputation reported to have entered the French lines.[63]

[The pocket in the back cover of this notebook held a photograph of Eddie's niece Robina aged about five. Robina was the daughter of Bob Giffard, Captain, Royal Artillery (Jack's twin) who had been killed in action in 1914].

8

W. E. Giffard's Diaries:
The First Notebook

5 December 1917
Left Victoria 7.35 a.m.[1] Good crossing but very cold. Left
Folkestone 10.30 arrived Boulogne 12.15 a.m. Having with
great difficulty collected our kit with aid of French porters,
awful consternation no one knew how to tell them to take it
to the cloakroom, which no one knew French for. Saved the
situation by 'take it to the cloakroom George' which was
immediately understod and complied with.

Lunch, tea and dinner at the Folkestone Hotel, very good
dinner. Won 20 frs at bridge and got into train at 11.15
p.m. Train left at 1 a.m. and

6 December 1917
we tried to sleep six in a carriage. But, as Bairnsfather[2] put
it, we had to get up and rest every now and then. Very cold
indeed, thankful I only had one leg to get cold in. Tony[3]
rather fed up, remarked it was a blinking sight nicer to be in
England wishing you were in France, than to be in France
wishing you were in England. Arrived Hazebrouck 6 a.m.
had breakfast and shave at Officers' Club. Tender arrived at
10 a.m. and took us to Bailleul 2nd Wing Hqrs.[4] Then Tony
and I went to 13th Section[5] at Swan Chateau[6] in time for
lunch. Went up in the afternoon but could see nothing. Hun

196

welcomed us by bombing from 6–7 also shelling Ypres well over our heads.

7 December 1917

First day at the war, breakfast in bed at 11 a.m. View dud but improving. Went up in afternoon, Hun plane came over but driven off by Archie.[7]

8 December 1917

Went up in the morning but view not good enough to shoot. Hun had a few shots at us but left off when we went higher.

9 December 1917

Dud view all day, messed about in chart room etc.

10 December 1917

Quite a good view, up with Skates who did several shoots. 6 Hun planes just over head, quite ready to jump, but they were in too much of a hurry, hotly pursued by five SE5s.[8]

11 December 1917

Very cold, no view all day; eat, played bridge and wrote some letters.[9]

12 December 1917

Misty, no view all day. What did you do in the Great War daddy? Eat, slept, and played bridge.

13 December 1917

Went up for an hour in the afternoon but very poor visibility.

14 December 1917

Dreamt last night I had received a large pile of letters —

awful nightmare. View dud all day, went into Bailleul in the afternoon with Stafford. Bought a flea bag, went to the 'Barn Owls', quite a good show. Had dinner at the Officers' Club. Everything looks as though the war were a permanency. Officers' Club lately and very tastily redecorated inside and out. Wine list in solid leather with 'Officers' Mess Bailleul' in heavy gilt printing.

Got back to find the dream was not a nightmare, but had come true. First letters since leaving England.

2/Lieut. W. E. Giffard, 1917.

15 December 1917
Very misty in morning, went up with Dreschfield and later with Tony. When with the latter, one of our aeroplanes returning home pretended he was a Hun and dived straight for us, awful funny joke, not appreciated at the time. More letters! Did first night work, up with Lardiner from 10 p.m. to midnight, took a few bearings.

16 December 1917
Very misty in the morning. Balloon went up in the afternoon. I went over and had tea at 'Company'. Hatch and Bradford came to dinner and stayed till tomorrow morning.

17 December 1917
Balloon re-rigged and new cable, had breakfast in bed at 11

a.m. Tried to get into Ypres but Hun was making it a bit too warm.

18 December 1917

Very cold and too strong a wind for the old sausage. Went and had tea at Officers' Club in Poperinge with the Doctor.

Two years ago today I shot my first woodcock at Olantigh.[10]

19 December 1917

Very misty. Jenkinson was up with an NCO when four bullets whistled through the basket. They lost no time in jumping and landed safely. Hun attacked the sausage four times and riddled it but by a miracle did not set it on fire. Archie opened up with great enthusiasm, but although the Hun was under 3000 feet they only succeeded in missing him but hit the balloon 3 times.

Gunner officer ran over to section and made anxious enquiries about the observers and the balloon. CO replied 'Oh yes observers are all right and the balloon wouldn't have been so bad if those blinking idiots with the archie had not hit it three times —? You are not an archie officer are you?' Silence meant consent and he was offered a drink. Jenks came over to tea.

20 December 1917

Thick fog no ballooning. Went into Ypres in the afternoon, and found Bob's grave[11] in excellent condition. Tony and I went over to No. 9 for dinner.

21 December 1917

And yet again a fog. Tony, Jenks and I went into Bailleul, saw a show and had dinner. Taking Jenks home to No. 9 we had to pass through Ypres. Got stuck on the outskirts after passing through and whilst waiting the Hun plonked four crumps into the town. Came back and whilst going from Ypres to here ½ mile, we heard five more go into the town, if we had been 5 minutes later either way, we might have got a puncture.

22 December 1917

Bitterly cold but good visibility, went up from 1 o'clock till dark on an empty stomach. Lot of wind, Smith evidently thought there were some fishes in the air, as he fed them liberally.

23 December 1917

Thick fog, nothing doing. Got two parcels and some Xmas letters. Dreschfield came to dinner.

24 December 1917

Went up about an hour with Smith and did some shoots, good visibility but basket was jerking about too much for accurate observation. Got more parcels and letters, and had several fellows to dinner. Chickens very excellent, also dates and chocolates.

Xmas Day 1917

I can imagine them saying 'poor fellows spending Xmas in France'. Well we had a dinner party of 14 and this was the menu:

> Hors d'oeuvres
> Oxtail soup
> Lobster Mayonnaise
> Roast Turkey with sausages
> Potatoes and Peas,
> Plum pudding (on fire)
> Fruit jellies
> Cheese straws

Coffee
'FIZZ'

I bet not many people at home had a dinner like that and in any case it is much easier for us to keep going than it is for them. We have nothing to worry us. Fritz did not bomb us for once.

Boxing Day 1917

If there is any place more likely to make one feel Christmasie than another, I should think it is a balloon on a windy day.

But Whelan and I were none the worse for being up for three hours in the afternoon. Got another parcel. Fritz started bombing again.

27 December 1917

Went up with Whelan for a couple of hours, not good enough to shoot, but spotted some active hostile batteries, we could not find, however, the fellow who was shelling us once every 5 minutes for the last hour we were up.

It's not a pleasant sensation being shelled in a balloon, especially when you see your next door neighbour shot down, give me a Hun plane any day.

28 December 1917

Orderly officer, seemed as though there might be a view so ordered the balloon out at 7.30.

Seemed to be a lot of wind so stopped the winch at 1500 feet and told them to take the tension.[12] '1000 kilos sir, and she's lifting the winch off the road sir.' Well, tell the balloon crew to sit on the winch; 1000 kilos and anything over 800 is supposed to be risky, 'Hello chart room, take the wind please.' '56 miles an hour, sir.' 'Put me on to the OC will you?' Told the OC the circs, what about it? 'For Lord's sake come down'. 'Hello, winch, haul down.' Five minutes later,

201

'Hello winch, have you started hauling down yet.' 'No, sir, the engine won't start, there's too much strain.' 'Well, put her into low gear and for Lord's sake haul down.' Took 25 minutes to get down from 1500, no more today, thank you.

29 December 1917

Thick fog; went for a walk, there and all the way back again! Jenks and Pearson came over to dinner. Got the piano into the mess and had a sing-song.

30 December 1917

Another fog, walked over to 'company' for tea, and went to No. 9[13] for dinner, they had just been brought down by 'Clockwork Charlie' consequently we made up for it with a cheery evening.

31 December 1917

Balloon went up for short time but too much wind. Huge crowd to dinner and concert afterwards. Saw the New Year in and heard our gunners and the Hun gunners paying each other the compliments of the season.

1 January 1918

Lot of wind; Tony went up; balloon very nearly broke loose before getting on to the winch. Practically no wind at 3000, but too foggy for shooting.

2 January 1918

Absolute dud day; went for a joy ride to fetch stores from Drugland[14] through Pop., Abeek, Steenvourde, back by 'Wing' and 'company'.

3 January 1918

A grand day. Whelan went up and did some shoots at 12 o'clock. Hun opened Clockwork Charlie on him and had a 'plane observing for him. The fifth shot cut the telephone cable and put 47 holes in the balloon, she came down quite gently and he did not have to parachute.

Patched her up and had her aloft within ¾ of an hour. Clockwork Charlie is getting too accurate, 4 out of the 7 balloons in our neighbourhood were shot down today. Two gunner officers from 381 HB came over to dine.

4 January 1918

Dud. Went over to 'company' to lunch with Tony. Whelan and I went to dinner with 381 HB in Ypres. Stafford went on leave. It's rather curious going out to dinner, one changes and has a wash and brush up, just as in civilised life, and we 'phone up to the camp and order the car to be ready at such and such a time, then you set off with a tin helmet and gas mask. Had quite a cheery evening with 381, it will make our work a lot easier if we get to know a few of these batteries, e.g. I have hatched a little scheme with 381 for the next fine day, the cunning of it being in overcoming the universal red tape which seems to abound in larger quantities out here than anywhere else.

5 January 1918

Completely dud, went for a stroll in the afternoon, had some gunners in to dinner.

6 January 1918

Dud again; went up with Whelan to have a look but it was quite hopeless; being 12th night, we burnt our few twigs of holly and 'so to bed'.

7 January 1918

The 2nd gunner guest arrived for his three day stay, very different from the first one. The first one, very much interested and very keen on going up in the balloon, although she

203

was hit as he was coming here. He went up and had an excellent view and I think went away with quite a good idea of the possibilities and limitations of balloon observation. This second one he is something h'awful, just like that, and refuses to go near the balloon. I hope it is a fine day tomorrow, I shall have great pleasure in taking him up at 7 a.m. if it is, as I am OO. Nothing doing today. Walmsley and 'Doc' came to dinner.

8 January 1918

Dud. Thank heaven, we had got our old balloon back, the last 10 days we have had an experimental one, and a blinking uncomfortable experiment it was. We blew the old one up this morning and then sent her up to see if she was alright, without anyone in her. She was quite alright, but she had not been up 20 minutes before 'Clockwork Charlie' made a damn good shot at her, but by a miracle she was not holed. Looks as though 'Clockwork Charles' has got our range pretty well, and I doubt if we stay up very long the next time we go up.

Two gunners came to lunch from A 330.[15]

9 January 1918

Snowing again and mighty cold. Went for a joy ride with Tony to Company, Mont Noir, Mont Rouge and Bailleul where we had tea.

10 January 1918

Excellent visibility but a gale like nothing on earth, all we could do to hold the sausage in bed.

Four invitations to go out to dinner tonight! Accepted the first which was to go with Whelan to 381 at Ypres gas works, had quite a good evening. I have been in and out of Ypres about a dozen times now whilst they have been crumping it, but have not had one near enough to call it near. However as we were walking back to the tender I went into a shell-hole which was not there when we went into dinner, and got soaked up to my knees.

11 January 1918

Quite clear early but too much wind. Then wind went down but rain came on. Went for a walk with Tony. Charlie and Lardiner came to dinner and left before breakfast tomorrow.

12 January 1918

Another poor day. Whelan went up in the morning but saw nothing. I went up in the afternoon with Tony and saw the same thing.

Another of those gunner blokes here. It seems the batteries each send the one they most want to get rid of. The last one made unpleasant noises with his tongue and teeth for about an hour after each meal. This one has not reduced that habit to quite such a fine art and does not keep on so long, but every little while there is a sound of mighty rushing waters in his throat and the next moment the cause thereof is sizzling on the fire.

13 January 1918

Tried to get the balloon up, but the winch skidded off the road into a ditch and took an hour to get it out again, by which time it was 'dud'. Just after we had got it out Charley arrived with a motor lorry with a crane on it. Went for a walk in the afternoon and dined at Company.

14 January 1918

Snowed all the morning, but delightful in the afternoon, no use for ballooning. Another gunner merchant arrived for his three days. He neither sucks his teeth nor spits and is very keen to go up in the balloon.

He also says that his battery has no faith in balloon observation, otherwise he seems to be a gentleman.

Well I hope we have a good day before he goes so that we can change his ideas.

15 January 1918

Very strong wind and some snow. Went over to dinner at Company, Hunter[16] more Hunnish than ever. Called out of bed at 1 a.m. to hold the balloon down, never seen such a wind, hung on to the balloon for an hour and half and then we got her more [or] less secure.

I never struck such a night, I think I was the only officer who did not finish up in a shell-hole.

16 January 1918

Still blowing a gale in the morning, but we went after lunch to test, but t'was no good. Had a concert at YMCA, Falck, Charley, Doc and Walmsley came to dinner at 2 p.m.[17]

17 January 1918

Snowed pretty well all day. Went to dinner with A/330, fellow who asked me, I know him quite well but I don't know his name, going to Blighty tomorrow on the same course as Eddie.[18]

Showed me how to make a very excellent rum punch.

18 January 1918

Raining, went for a ride with Doc and Walmsley. Went to dinner with Y1. Not allowed to use the tenders owing to thaw, so had to walk, and tumbled into umpteen shell holes.

19 January 1918

Quite a good day, balloon was up for eight hours and did quite a lot of shoots. Clockwork Charlie was very busy but he did not hole us, he did however shoot down 23, and 9, and broke 32's cable. Wind was blowing straight for Hun line and our planes strafed the balloon after they had jumped.

20 January 1918

Blowing a gale, wind order to put up in ballast and test tension, which I being OO did. I turned the wind-gauge on before putting her up, so that we could take the wind as well. When I had sent my report in, the Col rang up and asked how I had given strength of wind when he had told me to put up in ballast, adding something about guessing being bad practice. As if anyone could guess the strength of the wind at a 1000 ft! He seemed very surprised when I explained how it was done.

21 January 1918

Rained all day. Falck and Charley came to dinner.

22 January 1918

Quite good visibility but plenty of wind. Tony went up and we arranged some shoots, but he could not find the targets, so he came down and I went up to help him. We stayed up till dark and did a lot of shoots. In the evening the Col. rang up and congratulated Tony on his excellent day's work, rather amusing considering he had to be shown where the targets were. Clockwork Charlie was potting at us all day, but we diddled him, he shot down 9 and 23 again.

23 January 1918

Completely dud in the morning, but cleared a bit after lunch, so I went up to have a look. There were thick clouds at 1000 feet, so I went through them to 4000 ft,[19] it was quite hopeless as far as work goes, but worth seeing, clouds looked like a layer of cotton wool as far as one could see, but quite clear above them. When at 4000 a poor little mouse dropped out of the rigging past the basket, but I could not catch him to put a parachute on to him and he disappeared in the clouds below.

24 January 1918
Went for 3 days liaison with 39 SB at their rest billets in Ypres in what is left of the Rue de Paradis, now known as 'Paradise Alley'. Funny crowd, after dinner they asked me what I would like to do. I suggested bridge, they suggested dominoes, I suggested marbles and we did nothing.

25 January 1918
Went up to the guns, they were not very busy, nor was the Hun. Reduced to dominoes in the evening.

26 January 1918
Saw a balloon floating over towards the Hun about lunch time. Heard afterwards it was our balloon, cable shot away. Stafford and gunner who took my place did successful parachutes.

27 January 1918
Went home again and went out to dinner with Tony to No. 9.

28 January 1918
At last we are able to give the Hun a little of his own back. Got a battery to fire on the Hun balloons, Tony was up and they drove 3 of them down after a few shots, they weren't hit, merely got wind up. They wouldn't like the rule we have, not allowed to come down when you are being shelled, especially if they got it as much as we do. Went to tea with A Batt 330 Brigade, slapped a subaltern on the back and cheeryohed him and he turned out to be a colonel. However, all's well that ends well. Went to dinner at Hqrs 330 Bde.

29 January 1918

Orderly dog. Went up at 7.00 am and stayed up till 12 o'clock, did not know whether to have tea or lunch, so had both. Did some of the Hun balloon shooting, but they hauled down before we had got their range properly. However it is better to give than to receive.

30 January 1918

Went up with Whelan at 11 a.m. and stayed up till 4 o'clock. Drove two Hun balloons, but guns in our Corps could not reach any more of them. They retaliated but did not get very near us. We did several shoots and todays report was '16 targets were engaged by the Wing today'. Of these 7 were carried out by 13th KBS including five destructive counter battery shoots. Had a concert in the evening.

31 January 1918

Dud. Went to lunch at company and dinner at 330 Bde RFA.

1 February 1918

13th Section went out to rest, but Whelan, Tony and I stayed in with 36. Hopeless, confusion, I took on PMC and was told 36 would bring all provisions for first few days and was somewhat rushed when they turned up at 11 a.m. without a crumb or a drop.

2 February 1918

Awful dud section and Mess is spoilt by friction between certain members. Doc and Walmsley came to dinner.

3 February 1918

Balloon went dud and fell with Falck from about 1000 but it came down very slowly and no damage done.

4 February 1918

Tested balloon again, but she was worse than before and we got her condemned. Consequence — working on the new one till 10.30 p.m.

5 February 1918

Went up with Anderson, but could see nothing. Went to Bailleul in the afternoon to get some provisions. And went with Tony to 47 to dine.

6 February 1918

Had a new batman he is dud; greatest difficulty in getting him to leave my leg, he wanted to take it out and polish it or something. Being OO I went up to have a look but there was a ---- of a gale and we could see nothing, and the gunner who came up with me having relieved himself of his lunch and breakfast, and I should think last night's dinner as well, I decided to come down, but as the tension was 25 cwt before we started down, it looked rather like breaking away, however we did it alright. Half an hour later Wing rang up to say they thought the view had improved and we were to test it. They did not mention the fact that the wind had increased. I went up with Whelan and at 2000 the tension was 30 cwt and the wind over 60 m.p.h. and we could see less than before and so we came down again. The roughest journey I've ever had. Went to dinner with Doc and Walmsley.

8 February 1918

What a dud section this is, and still worse now, they have sent all our sergeants and all our riggers on leave the same day. No ballooning today h--- of a gale.

9 February 1918

Still blowing like nothing on earth and raining too. Doc and

Walmsley came to dinner and most people cleared off to bed at about 11 p.m. but Whelan and Walmsley and I went on chatting and we suddenly looked at our watches and found it was

10 February 1918

4.30 a.m. so we decided it was not worth while going to bed, so at 6.30 a.m. Walmsley supplied the horses and we went out for a ride. Still blowing too much to balloon.

11 February 1918

Dud again. Went into Bailleul to get some stores. Chambers our latest gunner guest came too. We went back to dinner with his battery.

12 February 1918

Obviously dud, but Wing ordered all balloons up, they only stayed up about 10 minutes as with clouds at 1000 ft, nothing could be seen. Went to dinner with 'A' Battery 330 Brigade.

13 February 1918

Nothing doing. Doc and Ketterel came in for farewell dinner as they are going south[20] tomorrow with 66 Div, we shall miss 330 very much.

14 February 1918

Dud. Lots of letters and parcels for my birthday.[21] We were eating some of Jenny's[22] caramel, when the Colonel rang up, and none of us could answer for some time. But luckily I have a large mouth.

Page and Stirk and Norquay came into dinner and we all gambled afterwards.

15 February 1918

Lots more parcels etc for my birthday. Skates came over to

collect all 13's belongings leaving us with absolutely no mess furniture or crockery. We are in an awful state, anyone would think there was a war on.

16 February 1918
Smith went up at 7 a.m. so I was pulled out to go in the chart room, since Anderson was only other officer here. Smith said he could see nothing, but mist might clear away any moment. I relieved him at 10.30 and found perfect visibility so asked him to get me some shoots. He could not for a long time and at 12.30 the telephone became dis.[23] So far I had been sitting up doing nothing for two hours with Clockwork Charlie having a go with his usual regularity every 5 mins. Smith seemed to think he could mend the phone from the ground so I had to put up with Clockwork Charlie for another hour and half without even a phone to comfort me. They finally pulled me down at 2 o'clock and mended the phone.

17 February 1918
Orderly dog — same sort of day, I went up at 6.30 and it was too misty to shoot, but looked as though it might clear at any moment. Smith relieved me at 10.30. It did not clear all day.

18 February 1918
Dud. I set off in a side-car to liaison with some batteries.

Foolish enough to think I could memorise the map, and did not bring one with me, so went sailing up Zonnebeeke road, nearly up to the trenches before I realized my mistake.

Visited various batteries and fixed up a number of shoots, excellent lunch with Chambers of 23 SB.

19 February 1918
Dud. Tadgell and I went into Bailleul to get some crockery

and cutlery for the Mess. Quite a successful expedition and found a place to get flour, unbeknownst.

20 February 1918

Dud. Tony and I took tender and went to liaise with batteries, quite an amusing and successful afternoon. In the evening Tony and I walked over to 47 for dinner.

21 February 1918

Quite a full day's ballooning. I took gunner up in the afternoon and we did several shoots, he was delighted to find how easily one can see the target, and thought OP's ought to be abolished. Falck returned from leave.

22 February 1918

No ballooning. I laid myself up doctor's orders — wanted to send me to hospital. Tony was called away to 25 for a fortnight.

23 February 1918

Still laid up, no ballooning and Laycock came to lunch and Walmsley to dinner.

24 February 1918

Quite dud. Tony had to go to 25 for a fortnight as they are short of officers. Went to 47 for dinner.

25 February 1918

Raining all day. Dreschfield and Wright came over to lunch.

26 February 1918

Looked possible early, so I went up at 7 o'clock. But could see nothing. I was just singing to myself 'When you are happy, friend of mine and all your skies are blue' when Clockwork Charlie put a nasty grey cloud just in front of me, so I quickly switched to the second verse 'When you are lonely friend of mine and all your skies are grey.' Charlie continued for another hour but did not hit anything and I came down at 10.30. Anderson went up later and had a very rough passage coming down and two of the crew got picked up and swung across the winch, but were not hurt.

27 February 1918

No ballooning. We have had a better lot of gunners lately. The latest one mentioned in his first five minutes that he was headmaster of a public school, I immediately felt great respect for him and nearly called him 'sir', but he seemed very little acquainted with an 'H' except where it was not wanted and I afterwards discovered that his public school was Cardiff Grammar School. Went into Bailleul for tea and dinner.

28 February 1918

Went up for about 3 hours waiting for visibility, how I hate waiting for visibility, especially when Clockwork Charlie does not bother to wait, as this morning when he put ten over at me, the last 4 or five were decidedly uncomfortable but he failed to puncture the blister or me, because he was just over each time. But he put the wind up me alright.

1 March 1918

No ballooning. Another gunner arrived, he asked me if I had any relations in Birmingham, as he remembered a fellow of that name who used to blow up tyres in a garage where he used to do the repairs.

2 March 1918

Alcock[24] went on leave, 3 days before his time, but I suppose I shan't get mine till Smith or Whelan come back. Went over to Hazebrouck and tead with 13.

214

3 March 1918

Another dud day. Went round batteries liaising and to 47 for dinner. Jenks got his leave.

4 March 1918

A battery I visited the other day did not believe in balloon observation. The Major said he didn't like shooting with them and for one thing they were too fond of giving OKs. However I finally extracted a promise that they would give me a trial the first fine day, whilst I undertook not to give OK without good reason. Well it came off today, it was on a couple of Hun guns in the remains of an isolated building. The battery shot toppingly and after a time I distinctly saw one shot demolish the building, so I sent OK. The Major immediately asked why I said it was OK and I told him, he said I could not see the house going up in brick dust at that distance.

A few minutes later there was another OK and there was literally nothing left of the position. I did not give another OK however and let them carry on. The next 3 or 4 shots I gave unobserved and after the 4th the Major asked what was happening, so I replied that there was no longer a target to observe on and he seemed more or less satisfied.

5 March 1918

Dud in the morning, but cleared a bit in the afternoon. Anderson did some shoots and Clockwork Charlie did some pretty good shooting on him. Two bits came through the Chartroom and one through Falck's dug out. Dined with 148.

6 March 1918

Quite dud all day. Got a photo taken of the shoot I did the other day, when I said the target disappeared, the photo proved my words to be correct, so I immediately took it

215

round to the battery, who are not so prejudiced against balloons as they were.

Dud early in the morning, but cleared later and I was up for about 3 hours doing some shoots. Clockwork Charlie started again and his tenth shot put a piece through the basket and two or three small bits through the blister for which I was thankful as I had to haul down and have them patched. Went over to Bailleul and tead with 7th Company, dined at 241. I don't love ballooning so much as I used to.

Not much bagging. Went to dinner with X 3[25] on the Menin road and told the tender to be back there at 10. He was not there so I started walking, which I did not relish as my leg was sore and the road in its best place was far worse than the Bath road[26] at its worst.

I had gone about 200 yards when the shoulder support[27] broke and it became absolute agony to walk so I sat down and waited. But the tender never came nor any vehicle of any description so I crawled on about 200 yards at a time. I had to get back as I was due to up the bag at 5.30 a.m. Also the Menin road is not a healthy spot to pass the night.

After two hours, I think the most painful I have ever spent, I got into Ypres and found a mule cart going in my direction. I gave the driver five francs. I was so bucked at getting a lift.

Very thick mist in the morning so did not up the bag. Had the delightful information that I may start on leave tomorrow, no we will say the 10th because tomorrow never comes. Laycock, Neal, and Walmsley came to dinner.

9

W. E. Giffard's Diaries:
The Second Notebook

26 March 1918

I said I wasn't going to keep a diary any more, but as I suppose this is the most colossal battle both in magnitude and importance that the world has ever seen, I think I will continue, although I may take no part in it.[1]

We had a fairly rough crossing and got to Calais about 6 in the evening. Here we were assured by a porter that the Hun had asked for an armistice, but we heard no more about it. Dined and slept at the Continental and Sauvage. Air raid during evening, one bomb demolished house next to Officers' club.

27 March 1918

Left Calais 10 a.m. Soon after leaving Hazebrouck we had the first glimpse of the war, when someone put his head out of the window and remarked, 'Damn good shot' and there was a poor old blister sitting up with the smoke of a shrapnel burst just above it, what a delightful welcome. Detrained at Poperinghe, which we found had been shelled in our absence.

Got back to Swan Chateau to find Lardiner in charge, Falck's nerves having apparently collapsed. They have

217

evidently been quite lively round here lately. Whelan and Sgt Whithers have each broken a leg, apparently got into an air pocket when parachuting and had a bit of a bump.

The drive perhaps leading to Walter Giffard's Swan Chateau, his 'home' at that time.

28 March–1 April 1918

A spell of those annoying days with mist and low clouds, both of which may clear away at any moment, and about once an hour a message comes from Wing, 'please test and report' so you up the bag and see nothing come down and then up again about an hour later, most aggranoying. Hun has been doing a lot of back area strafing and Ypres and Dickebush are always getting it now. Poor old Bailleul too is badly knocked about and there is no one left there now.

Tony and I thought we would go and see what his shooting was like on Dickebush, from a safe distance, but as we were passing Café Belge he dropped one short and we both decided we had seen enough.

Tony and I are getting rather fed up with our crowd; Lardiner of course is a jolly good fellow, but he never stops talking and he never talks anything but shop and it begins to nag after a while. Smith, well he is Smith of 1st Queens, 'nough said. Tadgell, well I suppose he can't help himself, but has such unfortunate ways, drinks his soup with an echo, you know, and speaks a dialect of his own. English I believe, but not easily understood. Consequence is every afternoon Tony and I start ringing up batteries until one of them asks us out to dinner. I have not been in to dinner yet since I came back, been to 381, 23, 241, 39, 198, Company, 18 and 25.

2 April 1918

Jackie's[2] birthday and I have not written well I cannot write tonight. Lardiner was called back to 13 last night and left me in charge.

Except for two intervals the bag has been up from 6 a.m. to 8 p.m. today. Tony went up at 6 and I was just going to relieve him at 9 o'clock when Clockwork Charlie opened up so of course he could not come down. However at 10 o'clock balloon was hit and we hauled down on top. There were only about a dozen holes and she was ready in ½ an hour, so I went up. Clockwork Charlie started again, but was shooting badly and I got his exact position behind Dadizeele, we immediately got a battery to fire on him, but before they were ready he put another over and holed the bag pretty badly in about 30 places. I very nearly jumped for it as I was at 4500 and I thought she might start falling before they could haul her down but she came down quite gently and I was glad I hadn't. She was ready again in an hour, but before going up I had taken the precaution to have something ready for Clockwork Charlie. A 12" How battery and 6" Mark 19 battery were all laid on our friend behind Dadizeele and ready to fire as soon as I could see the target. In order to see him really well I had to get to at least 4000 feet as he was at least 9 miles away and behind a wood. Consequence was he put 4 over at me as I was going up, but they were poor shots and only made me doubly sure of his exact position. Then the fun began both batteries shot toppingly and they were soon ranged, then they started battery fire and at times they simply obliterated Clockwork Charlie's position and also caused two explosions. What satisfaction, by Jove I did feel bucked then. I had just thanked the batteries and asked 2 of them to come round to dinner to celebrate the event, when I once more heard that unmistakable whistling and one burst just over me. I knew it was not our old friend because it had come from the wrong direction and 25 rang up to say they thought it had come from Menin. So I turned towards Menin and in a few minutes saw a flash, about 50 secs later the old bag had been hit in the nose. She did not seem so badly hit as she had been this afternoon, so I gave up the idea of jumping, suddenly when we were less than 1000 feet up I realized she was coming a bit too fast, it was too late to jump so I climbed into the rigging. It was very lucky I did as the basket came down with a great bump and took most of the shock and after a second or two I found I was quite OK. Well the gunners did not come to dinner as I got the balloon condemned, she has already been patched twice today and this last time she had some really bad holes. So we got a new bag which of course had to be inflated and tested at once. It is midnight now and the new bag is just ready to be tested so I must go and look on. I have been up since 5.30 in the bag for eight hours with two unexpected descents, oh yes I am deliciously tired, but I would rather it weren't quite so fine tomorrow.

3 April 1918

Just as fine as yesterday but not quite so much trouble. Smith went up early and Tony relieved him, but was shot down at lunch time. I went up when she had been patched and was not shot at at all. We did 3 more shoots than any other section today. Yesterday 25 did one more than us. I spent 7 hours in the bag today so I am going to bed.

4 April 1918

Another perfect day, and its the end of it thank heaven. Tony went up first thing and I relieved him at 9. Clockwork Charlie started at about 10 o'clock and continued shooting badly, but I could not get his exact position, miles away somewhere behind Menin. Finally at 3 o'clock he hit the blister, but not badly and she never looked like falling. After she had been patched (5th time we have been hit in 3 days, and I have been the unfortunate one 3 times) Smith went up but was unmolested. We did most shoots again today.

5 April 1918

Another fine day, bag was up for 14 hours and would you believe it, was not shot at at all. I spent 7 hours aloft making my total for the last 4 days, 28 hours. Capt Laycock came round to dinner and has promised Tony and I will get our wings on the 15th (only obtainable once a month). Just missed the hat-trick, 18 Section did one more shoot than us today. Thank heaven it looks like rain tonight.

6–10 April 1918

Lardiner came back on the 6th and brought 13 Section to relieve 36 who go to Hazebrouck. Tony and I stayed with 13. Very difficult to get definite news of the south but it seems quite satisfactory, they are apparently expecting an attack up here. Absolutely dud these days, and we spend most of the time liaisoning with batteries. Hun attacked at

Kemmel today (10th) and 25 Section had to retreat in a hurry and had to burn the balloon.

11 April 1918

Heavy bombardment all last night and Hun attacked at Gheluvelt this morning. Impossible to balloon owing to mist. Could not tell what was happening in the morning. At 8 p.m. we got orders to deflate the bag and pack up everything to go to St Omer at once. Everyone had to get down to it for all they were fit. Got shelled more or less all the time and the roads behind were being properly strafed. Laycock came round and went to Lardiner with a most alarmed expression, and said Tony and I were not just seeing that the men were loading the gas-tubes[3] on to the lorries, but we were actualty lifting them ourselves, talking absolute nonsense and roaring with laughter all the time, had we had too much to drink?

However we continued to laugh and be mistaken for drunkards. We got away with everything at 1 a.m. and no vehicle was hit on the road and we only had about 6 men wounded altogether.

12 April 1918

Arrived St Omer 6 a.m., unpacked and looked for billets all day, packed and stood by all night.

13 April 1918

Here are we in ignominious safety 30 miles behind the line doing nothing. Surely everyone can be of some use at a time like this when it is touch and go whether the Hun will break through or not. Balloons are no good in a retreat, granted, but they say the Hun has got Bailleul already (used to be 10 miles behind our position) surely anyone would be some use in the firing line. With these arguments Tony and I went to the Colonel today and asked if we might take our machine guns and see if we could be any use in the line, but he refused, and said balloons will soon be in the line again.

St Omer was bombed tonight and several houses, including one directly opposite our billet, demolished.

14 April 1918

Retreated another 20 miles to Desvres to unload stores.

15–18 April 1918

Unloading stores at Desvres, we didn't get to bed on 14th at all, and since then no one has had more than 4 hours sleep per night.

Just what would happen when we have got a most priceless billet, with a delicious bed which simply asks you to lie down and sleep forever. Tony and I had a most amusing time getting a billet, he knows about as much French as I do, or I know no more than he does whichever way you like to put it, either way it means damn little. At one place when they refused to understand us at all, I tried in desperation *'nous ne savons pas où layer les têtes'*, but they couldn't even understand that.

We ought to have had our wings by now, but we are no longer under the Col, so Laycock[4] has no one to recommend us to.

Just heard Tony and I are to go back to 36, I believe they are just north of Bailleul, so we ought to see something, but I wish we were going with 13, 36 are a rotten lot.

19 April 1918

Last night Laycock came upon Tony and I on top of a railway truck helping the men to unload stores, as one of us had just said something silly at which both us and most of the men were laughing, so I asked Laycock if he thought we had been 'at the bottle again'. No he did not think that, as it seemed to him we were always in the same state, but he added that we were there for the purpose of seeing that the men worked and not to work ourselves. I suggested that the men might feel more inclined to work if they saw us working, than they would be if we looked on with our hands in our pockets, and he seemed to think it quite a good idea. We stood by all day and finally the tender came for us at 9.30 p.m. and we arrived at 36 Section at Esquelbecq at

20 April 1918

3 a.m. this morning. They still do not consider the line steady enough for balloons and we have a meteorological expert with us, whom we take up at dawn, noon and sunset in all posible weather so I expect we shall have some lively rides.

21 April 1918

Had a bath! in Wormhoudt. Blowing the deuce of a gale and it was impossible to get the balloon up at dawn or noon. At sunset it seemed to have gone down a bit and Whitcombe said he must go up if possible. So he and I ascended. When we got to 500 feet however the bag was swinging over and nose-diving nearly to the ground on each side so we were ordered down for which neither of us was sorry.

22 April 1918

I have never before realized how cold it can be up aloft, it is warm now to what it used to be in January, but now that we are meteorological balloon we a take a thermometer up with us and this evening at 4000 feet it was 10° below freezing point.

23 April 1918

Heard the cuckoo for the first time this year, quite a decent day.

24 April 1918

Dropped a brick today. Went to Wormhout to get some money from the Field-Cashier who was advertised to be there at 10.15. I was still waiting for him with a few others at 11 o'clock, when a fellow came up and said 'Field Cashier'? So, I said 'no, he hasn't come yet; we've been waiting for the old blighter for ¾ hour already.' With much stuttering and many apologies for being late, he said 'I am the old blighter.'

25 April 1918

Heard today poor Old Doc, the MO of 330 Bde, is missing, he was a good fellow. I do hope he is alright. A year ago today I joined as a cadet at Farnborough.

26 April 1918

A Canadian Colonel came over today and said he wanted to go up in the bag. I was only officer in and I told him we had been warned not to go up as there was thunder about. He did not seem to think that mattered and in the end persuaded me to take him up. When we were up, he asked if he might smoke. I told him we were strictly forbidden to. Well, he said is there much risk. I said you would not have much time to jump if it caught fire from below, and nine times out of ten it would catch fire. Well, he said perhaps this will be the tenth and immediately lit a cigarette. I got awful wind up but all was alright.

27 April–10 May 1918

Went to Mary Capell aerodrome and demolished hangars. I have taken over meteor again, and there is apparently nothing for us to do, but to do manual labour. Not very *bon*, there is nothing to do when you have finished work and nowhere to go. We get a good many aeroplanes landing here for various reasons. Yesterday two fellows came down in SE5's. One had got over 30 Huns and the other had been out 5 weeks and got 8 Huns. Heard that Tony and I had got our 'wings',[5] we put them up today, Tony said he had got a stiff neck from continually looking to see if they were still there. Tony and I have been over to dine with Jenks and Pearson at 9 once or twice, last night the Colonel was there, first time I had seen him since I came out — practically 6 months — and I am sure he had not the slightest idea who I was last night.

11 May 1918

Heard this morning that I was wanted to go to 6th Coy for 'a day or two' whatever that means, to take the place of their recording officer who has gone sick. So here I am, Captain Forrest is a very good sort, and so is the Doc as far as he goes, but he only goes to about 3 ft 6 in.

12 May 1918

I rather like this job for a change. You go up in a bag when you feel inclined, and if you don't feel inclined you needn't go at all. Forrest annoyed a fellow in the Guards very much this morning. We were watching the balloons go up and this fellow came up. The sort of person who looks as though his name ought to be Vere de Vere, and when he can't think of anything else to say, he says Eh What, or by way of variation What! What eh! Well this morning he said 'I say should awfully like to do a jolly little parachute in one of your jolly balloons, eh what! What! What! eh!' to which Forrest replied 'We've got some work to do, Honey.' He did not like the 'Honey' at all.

13 May 1918

There is an old dug-out living with us here, a colonel, area commandant. He spent a long time last night bemoaning the fact that his son had just lost his leg below the knee. He did

not take any notice of what anyone said, and was fully
convinced that it were almost better to have been killed. 'But
you fellows do not realize what it means to lose a leg, he is
absolutely finished.' I suggested that he did not realize what
one could do with a leg. Then he asked for it, and he got it
right in the neck. 'What on earth do you mean? You say he
will be able to do anything, what do you mean?' 'Well, sir, I
shot my leg off six years ago, and I know I can do anything
within reason, and what is more your son at least has the
consolation that he lost his in the war.' He is a dear old thing
the colonel, but he was quite dumbfounded then, and ever
since has been asking me what his son will be able to do.

14 May 1918

Blazing hot again, it really is glorious weather, but I don't
suppose I should think so if I was with a section, it can be
too fine then.

15 May 1918

Still hot, I wish there was somewhere to bathe. Went over to
dine with Tony and Smith, who are now at 32 Section. I
expect I shall join them, but according to Baker, 'Not for a
day or two'.

16 May 1918

A new Recording Officer arrived and I went to 30 Section to
'up the bag'. Forrest asked me why I did not apply for RO's
job permanently as he was sure I would get it if I did. But I
do not think it is playing the game.

17–23 May 1918

Same every day. One of us goes up for about an hour at
dawn, which is 3.45 a.m. these days. Then it is usually misty
until 11 or 12 when we are up until 9 p.m. Not much
excitement so far. A Hun plane came over just as we were

reaching the ground the other night and tried to bomb us but failed.

24 May–1 June 1918

I have hardly met anyone since I was at 6 Coy who has not told me I am a d--- fool for not applying for the Recording Officer's job. The Doc says I ought not to be allowed to balloon and everyone seems to think I ought to have a job on 'terra firma'. Well, I've had my fill of ballooning, lately, but I am not going to apply for the job. The Hun burnt five balloons immediately to the north of us today, but was brought down before he reached us. The old blighter, not content with burning the balloons followed the observers down in their parachutes firing at them. Poor old Miller was killed and some others, I have not heard who or how many were wounded. There were 11 parachutes in the air at once. I never liked night work, but now I hate it, I never liked bombing, although one gets used to it, when he is over you for 4 hours on end nearly every night. But what I hate most of all is a combination of the two. Last night I was up in the bag from 11 p.m. until 2 a.m. and the Hun was over bombing all the time. We do not go above 2000 feet at night so there is not much likelihood of the Hun attacking you even if he saw you, but the bombs sound most horribly close as they go whistling past you, and what with 'Archie' and the machine gunners firing wildly at the Hun, when you know they can't see you, it is not over pleasant.

2 June 1918

Capt Forrest asked me today if he might apply for me to be his Recording Officer.[6] I suppose I still had the 'wind up' after last night, anyway in a weak moment I told him that if I was offered the job I would accept it.

I slipped getting out of the telephone lorry this evening and have got a little water on the 'knee'.

3 June 1918

Hun burnt three more balloons today, he came for us and Brooks parachuted successfully but the Hun did not burn the balloon. One blessing about my knee, I can go to bed at night knowing I shall not have to get up at 3.30 a.m., but I think it will be nearly well tomorrow.

4 June 1918

'Nough said, I go on leave tomorrow.[7]

Appendix: Sydney Giffard's Letter from Gallipoli

May Day 1915

My Dear Dada,

I am afraid I have not written for some time, but I told you not to expect a letter and I can get no postcards. You will probably have seen of our operations in the paper. The landing was a fine show and captured German officers said they could not have believed it possible. It was very sad losing my major about the third day and Booth a subaltern in the battery was badly wounded. We were the first artillery to get ashore. It is a very interesting operation and far more so than that latterly in France. I am now commanding the battery. Brooke is all right and I have got another subaltern instead of Booth. The climate is ideal except that for the first three or four nights I had no coat or blankets and no sleep. Otherwise I am as fit as usual but should like you to send out some more tobacco as I lost my stock. There are none of the comforts of France fighting but the climate makes up for a lot.

Best love to all

Yr affect son

Sydney

* * *

An enquiry from Jack Giffard elicited the following letter from another Old Marlburian gunner in Gallipoli:

22 May 1915

Dear Jack,

Just got your letter of 8th & have been to see Campbell who now commands 17th Brigade. He tells me young Brook has written about your brother, but as he himself has been wounded, not seriously, I will tell you what I know about it, or rather what I have heard from Campbell.

On May lst about 10 p.m. an attack was begun along the whole of our front. The Batteries which had been landed, viz B, Y, 13th & 26th were in action about 600 or 700 yds in rear of our front trenches, & the observing stations were in the case of 17th bde about 40 yds in rear of the front trench, in a dug out. The attack continued all night & at one time the situation seemed to be very serious. Col. Smith & Morgan were found behind the infantry trench, some way to the left of their Obs. Stn., & the supposition is that they had gone out to try & find out what was happening. About 4 a.m. a counter attack was delivered by the French, & the Turks had to retire, during which time we were able to give them a pretty hot time.

When they had gone back about 800 yards on our right front & more in our immediate front they got down into their trenches & stopped the counter attack.

Your brother, who was commanding the 26th Battery, (Pattison had been killed & Booth wounded the evening before) was standing up in his dug out looking for targets about 5.40 a.m. & had just turned round to say he couldn't see any Turks, when a rifle bullet hit him in the left temple. He was taken back to the beach, after being dressed, about two miles & a half back & taken off to a Hospital Ship, where he died the same evening, & was buried at sea, I believe, but am not absolutely certain.

231

I'm sorry I can't give you fuller details. That was a bad night, at least I don't want another like it.

I needn't tell you how sorry I was to hear the news next day. I knew him for a bit in India when we were doing a veterinary course together, & of course at Leamington.

I can't tell you much about this show, we are digging & sapping at the moment but hope to get a move on soon.

With deep sympathy,

Yrs,

Claude Daubeny

Notes

Chapter 2: Jack Giffard's Diary

1. Jack's battery, L Battery, Royal Horse Artillery, had been stationed at Aldershot, moving by road to Southampton to embark, a large part of the journey after dark.
2. Major the Honourable W. D. Sclater-Booth commanded the battery. Lieut. J. D. Campbell was a near contemporary of Jack Giffard.
3. 'I' refers to I Battery, RHA, headquarters probably of the First Cavalry Brigade.
4. Anchoring off Grand Dogger sounds rather hazardous, but presumably the German High Seas Fleet was known not to present an immediate threat.
5. Judging by the time of reaching Boulogne, the ship had lain at anchor for some hours during the night.
6. Jack's companion on his visit to the town was Captain E. K. Bradbury, who had joined L Battery recently as second in command after a tour of duty with 42 Field. Like Jack, he was an Old Marlburian. He was to be awarded the VC posthumously after the Néry battle.
7. Jack was orderly officer.
8. The reported sudden death of Jimmy Greison (*sic*) was evidently that of General Sir James Moncrieff Grierson, KCB, CVO, CMG, who had been GOC-in-C, Eastern Command since April 1912. He died near Amiens, see Introduction, p. 2.
9. General E. E. H. Allenby (later Field Marshal the Viscount Allenby) commanded the cavalry division.
10. Brigadier General C. J. Briggs, CB, commanded the First Cavalry Brigade. It consisted of the 2nd and 5th Dragoon Guards and the 11th Hussars, with L Battery. The division had two brigades of horse artillery. L were with I Battery in 7 Brigade RHA (Lieut.-Col. N. F. Birch) with its brigade ammunition column.
11. Aborge here may be a version of Obourg, where the canal crossing was a key feature and the station was the scene of a famous stand by the 4th Battalion Middlesex Regiment in one of the opening actions at Mons on 23 August.

12. They must have been ready to move at 4.00 a.m. because the intention was to send them to support the left of the British front, where they marched in the evening after a diversion to meet a threat on the British right.

13. East of Bray, beside the road to Péronnes, there is an inscription on a stone commemorating the firing of the first British artillery round of the war, by E Battery, RHA, on this day.

14. The Dragoon Guards were in the Second Cavalry Brigade, commanded by Brigadier General de Lisle (see diary for 24 August), with the 9th Lancers and the 18th Hussars.

15. The bleak forest was presumably the Bois de Colfontaine.

16. M must have been Marston (see diary for 24 August).

17. Sunday, the day on which it became clear that the German armies advancing around Mons outnumbered the British Expeditionary Force by about four to one, and that the BEF was equally severely outgunned. At General French's meeting in the Chateau de la Haie, with Generals Haig (I Corps), Smith-Dorrien (II Corps), Allenby, Robertson and Murray, the outline plan was agreed for the great retreat.

18. It was not surprising that L Battery waited for orders.

19. The main action described in Jack's diary for this day was selected as one of two 'incidents near Audregnies' for commendation by Major General Sir Frederick Maurice in his book *Forty Days in 1914* (Constable, 2nd edition, 1920, p. 99). His account is as follows: 'At this time when the flank attack of the German Fourth Corps had reached its full development a column of German infantry, almost certainly not less than a regiment of three battalions, was just debouching to attack, when "L" Battery RHA came into action behind a hedge 2000 yards from them, and, almost unaided and under heavy and continuous fire from not less than four enemy batteries, kept them at bay for nearly three hours, finally withdrawing without the loss of a gun, when almost all its ammunition had been expended.' General Farndale records that 'L Battery ... galloped into action behind the Norfolks ... did great execution, bursting its shrapnel low with terrible effect. Almost unaided, the battery drove this mass of German infantry back' and quotes Major Tom Bridges of the 4th Dragoons as having noted 'two British guns firing away at the advancing German hordes as steadily as if they had been on the range of Okehampton'. In his summary of this action, General Farndale writes, 'Though the Norfolks lost over two hundred men and the Cheshires nearly six hundred, the cavalry, these two battalions, L Battery RHA and 119th Battery RFA had checked the advance of a German Corps, so saving the left flank of the British Army. Such was the indomitable spirit of the Regiments and Batteries of the BEF.'

20. For de Lisle's brigade, see note 14 above for 22 August 1914.
21. Later Major J. E. Marston, DSO, MC.
22. Villers Pol is the place at which Jack's line of retreat in 1914 is crossed by Eddie Giffard's line of advance towards the end of the war in 1918. Outside the church there is a plaque inscribed 'La Société des Anciens Combatants a leurs comarades Anglais'.
23. Lieut. L. F. H. Mundy whose immediately previous posting seems to have been with the same unit, 42 Field, as that from which Captain Bradbury had come to join L Battery.
24. The South Lancashires were in Brigadier General McCracken's brigade, in the third division, which was commanded by General Hamilton. General Maurice's book (see above) described how 'von Der Marwitz's cavalry and the right column of the German Fourth Corps caught up an infantry rearguard of the British Third Division holding a position just North of Solesmes' and how the Wiltshires and South Lancashires and 'a battery of artillery' gained time for congestion on the roads to be cleared.
25. There was a gap between Smith-Dorrien's and Haig's corps because the state of the roads through the forest of Mormal forced their lines of retreat apart, on either side of it, the former moving through Le Cateau, the latter through Landrecies. The cavalry division covered the gap.
26. John here is Campbell. A Section in the RHA was usually two 13-pounder guns, and their teams.
27. Major Mullins (*sic.* could it have been Mullens?) was of the 4th Dragoon Guards.
28. From the afternoon of this day, the German attack lost some of its momentum.
29. The fifth division, commanded by General Sir Charles Fergusson, had been on the left of Smith-Dorrien's corps, on the line between Mons and Condé, and had come under overwhelmingly heavy attack at the outset, both from the front and from the left flank.
30. There are a few very old apple trees still around the village of Berlancourt.
31. Baillie is usually spelt Bailly.
32. The officer lost by the 4th Dragoon Guards this day was Lieut. O. B. Sanderson.
33. There is a fine house by the river, which now contains the *mairie* of Choisy-au-Bac, and another large place above it, just to the north, with grounds running down to the Aisne. The church contains a monument to a M. Binder who was mayor a few years before the Great War.
34. On First Cavalry Brigade, see note 10 above.
35. Gunner H. Darbyshire was also on 'the other gun', and Driver Osborne, both of whom received decorations for their part in the

action. The former's account of it is quoted in Lyn MacDonald's book *1914*. VCs were awarded to Captain Bradbury (posthumously) to Battery Sergeant Major Dorrell and to Sergeant Nelson. The BSM became a lieutenant colonel and survived the war. The sergeant was promoted to Major D. Nelson but did not survive. In his book *Riding the Retreat*, Richard Holmes records that Nelson's grave is at Lillers. He also writes that 'soon Lt. Giffard's gun was also silenced, its detachment wiped out.'

36. There are memorials in the village of Néry to L Battery and to the 2nd Dragoon Guards, the Queen's Bays. The latter quotes the famous dictum 'The Battle of the Marne was won at Néry.' L Battery lost five officers (that is, all who were on the spot) and over 40 men killed or wounded in a matter of minutes, and 150 of its 228 horses.

37. Lieut. C. H. Champion de Crespigny, 2nd DG.

38. Thomas Hinde quotes a terrible account of Captain Bradbury's wounds and death in his book on Marlborough College. Accounts of the battle are also given by General Farndale, whose *History of the Royal Regiment of Artillery, Western Front 1914–18* includes a sketch map of Néry; and notes that 'Lieutenant Giffard was wounded but recovered'; and by Major A. F. Beche, RFA, in a collection entitled *First World War Roll of Honour, Royal Artillery*; also in an article of May 1919 in the *Journal of the RUSI*, BSM Dorrell himself provided sketches of the positions that were used in Wilson's *The Great War*, a periodical publication still available in bound volumes. French accounts of the Néry battle include one by Capitaine de Labouchese, who was present. This account, translated by Major A. J. R. Lamb, himself awarded the DSO for his crucial role in the battle, in bringing the machine guns of the Queen's Bays into action with great effect, was published in *Cavalry Journal* in September 1935. General Lord Norrie lectured on the battle at the RUSI.

39. On Sclater-Booth, see note 2 above. Though Jack had no means of knowing exactly what happened, Richard Holmes (see above) records that Sclater-Booth, on his was back to the battery from brigade headquarters, 'was knocked down and disabled'. Another account adds that he lay unconscious for five hours where he fell before being resuscitated. He gave further distinguished war service and retired some years after the war as brigadier-general.

40. The First Cavalry Brigade's brigade major was Captain J. S. Cawley (not Calley), 20th Hussars. (Jack's spelling of this name would be accounted for by his familiarity with Wiltshire neighbours, the Calleys of Burderop Park.)

41. On Briggs, see note 10 above. He retired in 1923 as Lieut.-General Sir C. Briggs, KCB, KCMG.

42. The park at Baron is probably much as it was (see illustration).
43. The things hidden in the rafters included Jack's diary.
44. Captain W. B. Warrington, MD, RAMC, was an officer in the Territorial Army.
45. Lieut. J. G. A. Butler, 1st Life Guards, was promoted to captain in November 1914.
46. Babbles was Jack's wife Margaret (née Long). The eldest of their four daughters, Violet, was born in February 1915.
47. Henry, eldest of the six sons of Henry Rycroft and Cecily Giffard of Lockeridge House, had joined the Royal Navy as a cadet in 1895, and was one of the youngest captains RN by the end of the Great War.
48. The diary's question about Marshal Joffre's strategy was apt, since the turning of the tide at the Marne is often judged to have started on that day.
49. Captain W. G. F. Renton of the 1st Dragoon Guards, the King's or KDG. On the sugar factory, see diary for 31 August 1914.
50. The 'big victory at Meaux' would have referred to one of the most decisive actions in the Battle of the Marne, in which the BEF played a worthy and successful part.
51. Near the harbour at Le Havre, by the Musée des Beaux Arts, a feature on the shoreline is still known as l'Anse Frascati.
52. Colonel Sir Mark Sykes, Bart., MP, whom Jack night have known when both were soldiering in South Africa.
53. Dad is H. R. Giffard.
54. Muriel is perhaps Mrs Campbell-Laverton, sister-in-law of Dr Walter Maurice, on whose medical advice Lockeridge House always relied (see also Introduction, and *The Marlborough Doctors* by T. R. Maurice, Alan Sutton, 1994).
55. Mrs Robert Long was Babbles's mother (see note 44 above) and Lady Scobell was one of her Wiltshire neighbours.

Chapter 3: Eddie's Diary: The First Notebook

1. He was seen off by his father, H. R. Giffard (D), his sisters Polly, May and Maud, and by his brother Jack with his wife Margaret (née Long).
2. His eldest surviving sister, Cicely, was living in Weymouth with her three young sons, having lost her husband, Commander T. H. M. Maurice, RN, on 27 May that year, when his ship was destroyed by enemy action at Sheerness.
3. This is the only direct criticism of any party of British soldiers made in the whole diary.

4. Though his brothers' reputations may have counted for something, his posting to the Guards Division surely implies that Eddie had done pretty well in training.
5. Probably Lieut. F. D. Swinford, RA.
6. OMs are Old Marlburians.
7. W. E. Mann, DSO, was staff captain and later brigade major, RA.
8. On J. F. Ireland, see diary for 31 July 1917. Later Captain, MC and a renowned games player.
9. D. Le P. Trench, MC, was brigade major, RA.
10. Eddie's spelling of proper names is uncharacteristically casual. Brigadier General A. E. Wardrop, CMG, was in command of the Guards Division Artillery from September 1915 to February 1916, then BGRA, XIV Corps, and Major General GOCRA Third Army. The twins of whom he spoke kindly were Eddie's brothers Bob and Jack.
11. On Toppin, see note Chapter 4 note 9. The battery was D Battery, 76th Brigade, RFA.
12. Lieut. J. G. Dutton was awarded the MC in June 1916.
13. Observation post, from which forward observation officers were in touch by field telephone with gun batteries.
14. Dutton. See note 12 above.
15. X was the section of two or three guns from his battery for which he was observing. As liaison officer, he was responsible for communications between his battery and the infantry they were supporting.
16. Semple seems to have left Eddie's brigade. Captain R. E. W. Semple, MC, died of wounds on 5 November 1918.
17. The CRA was presumably Wardrop, see note 10 above. He is frequently mentioned in the diary.
18. Buzzard cake was perhaps a Lockeridge speciality.
19. Winston C. Churchill, having left the Admiralty, and the government after the failure of the Gallipoli expedition, went out to the Western Front for 18 months commanding a battalion of the Royal Scots Fusiliers. He returned to the Cabinet in Lloyd-George's government as Minister of Munitions in 1917.
20. This suggests that Eddie had gone out to Australia in about 1909.
21. The Rebbecks owned the bakery and the inn (The Who'd 'A Thought It) in Lockeridge, and members of the family worked in various capacities with the Giffards.
22. CDQ was clearly a pre-arranged call for fire.
23. Pipsqueaks were rounds from German guns of small calibre and recognizable from their incoming noise: cf. 'whizzbangs', 'whistling willies'.
24. Lieut.-Col. (later Colonel) J. V. Campbell, DSO, won the VC on 15 September 1916, leading his battalion and rallying them with his

hunting horn in the famous attack by the Guards Division on the Somme in the battle of Bapaume. He was also later made CMG.

25. Lieut.-Col. P. A. McGregor, DSO.

26. See illustration of Rue Tilleloy's quiet appearance in 1996.

27. 2/Lieut. L. V. Atkinson

28. General Cary was probably General de Langle Cary, who commanded the French Fourth Army during the battles of the Marne and the Aisne.

29. The clothes were presumably additional kit to help cope with deteriorating conditions.

30. This shell was the only 'short' mentioned in the diary, those on 14 January 1918 being only rumours.

31. This fraternizing was probably not one of the most famous instances at Christmas 1915.

32. Ernie was one of Eddie's many Maurice brothers-in-law, and was godfather to Walter Giffard.

33. Collaroy is the name of the sheep station in New South Wales originally owned by the Hamilton (Eddie's mother's) family, at which Eddie had been working until the outbreak of war. The diary never mentions it again.

34. A reconstructed building of this name was still to be seen in 1996 just north of the Rue Tilleloy, see illustration.

35. Eddie misspelled Hougoumont, which no doubt was named after the farm at Waterloo, famously defended by the Coldstream Guards in 1815.

36. Baseden, Gardiner-Waterman, Sheridan and Scott-Deacon were from various batteries, probably of 76th Brigade, RFA. For Scott-Deacon, see also diary for 31 July 1917. The first name here may have been intended for that of 2/Lieut. H. Baseden, the second was probably Lieut. J. F. Sheridan. Major Gardiner-Waterman was temporarily in command of 61st Brigade. RFA at about this time.

37. Coal boxes were shells, nearly 250 lbs in weight, fired by the German 8.27 howitzer, which exploded with dense black smoke.

38. Paul Methuen:(1886–1974) son and heir of Field Marshal Lord Methuen of Corsham Court; country neighbour, up the Bath road from Lockeridge, who had also been at Horris Hill Preparatory School with Eddie. He was serving with the Scots Guards as a lieutenant. (Jack Giffard had been on Lord Methuen's staff in South Africa. See also *Fourteen Friends* by James Lees-Milne.)

39. For Cicely, see note 2 above.

40. For Burston, see diary for 24 February 1916.

41. This was the day of one of the heaviest raids on Britain by airships during the Great War, when bombs dropped by six or seven

zeppelins, flying mostly over East Anglia and parts of the Midlands, killed more than 60 people and injured over 100.

42. The Paddington (Great Western) Hotel was much as it is now.

43. From the main Great Western line to the southwest, you changed at Savernake for Marlborough, where you arrived at the higher-level station (the lower one was for the line to Swindon and Cirencester).

Chapter 4: Eddie's Diary: The Second Notebook

1. Robina is Bob Giffard's daughter. See also note at end of complete diary.

2. Two or three of the six guns in the battery. Thus, there are references to left and right sections, and occasionally to a centre section.

3. Henry, his eldest brother, later Captain, RN, writing from his ship, probably at sea.

4. Brigadier General Wardrop, see Chapter 3, note 10, of above.

5. The GOC was Major-General G. T. P. Feilding, CB, CMG, DSO. F. M. Lord (then Sir John) French had mentioned him in dispatches for his part in the retreat from Mons, as the lieutenant colonel commanding the third battalion, Coldstream Guards, and had commanded 1st Guards Brigade from August 1915 until January 1916. He became GOC Guards Division on 3 January 1916, and stayed with it until 30 September 1918. Later became Major-General Sir Geoffrey Feilding, KCB, KCVO. Eddie almost never spells his name correctly.

6. For Ireland, see Chapter 3, note 8 above.

7. Batten-Poull (sic). J. A. Batten Pooll, MC, late of the 5th Lancers, was Staff Captain, RA, at divisional headquarters, from 13 January to 19 December 1916.

8. The Revd W. P. G. McCormick, DSO, was senior Church of England chaplain to the forces with the Guards Division from December 1915 to May 1917. He was widely admired, not least by Eddie; see diary for the following day and later references.

9. Major Robertson was perhaps from another battery in the brigade. Toppin had evidently been promoted, presumably to command D/76. See diary for 14 November 1915. As Major S. M. Toppin, he was in command of C Battery, 61st Brigade RFA when Eddie joined it in May 1916, and temporarily in command of the brigade.

10. Appleby of 42nd Field, a renowned battery, active until the 1990s.

11. Perhaps Major Robertson, see note 9 above.

12. On 27 March a number of powerful explosions were set off near here, in mines tunneled under one of the strongest German positions round Ypres. The resulting huge craters later changed hands repeatedly in bitter fighting.

NOTES

13. The new niece was his brother Jack's second daughter, Sybelle or Sybil, born on 8 April 1916, and baptized at St Peter's church in Marlborough.
14. On Bob's grave, see Chapter 8 note 11.
15. For Wardrop, see Chapter 3, note 10 above.
16. Eddie's late mother's sister, Laura Hamilton. See Chapter 9 note 2.
17. Perhaps 2nd Lieut., later Captain A. McQueen.
18. For Burston, see diary of 24 February 1916.
19. Brigadier General W. Evans, DSO, had succeeded General Wardrop in command of the divisional artillery at the beginning of March and remained with them until 27 May 1917.
20. Probably the Revd H. E. Hubbard.
21. General Townshend had been forced to surrender at Kut-El-Amara on 29 April for lack of supplies. There was much criticism of the British and Indian governments for having failed to avert what was widely regarded as an unnecessary disaster.
22. Talbot House (or Toc H) is still there to visit. See also diary for 15 May 1916.
23. Gunter was for cake what Fortnum & Mason were for many other desirable supplies.
24. The Battle of Jutland, in which Eddie's cousin Midshipman Robin Giffard, RN, son of Admiral G. A. Giffard, was lost, had been fought on 31 May.
25. The sinking of HMS *Hampshire*, which struck a mine off the Orkneys, with the loss of Field Marshal Lord Kitchener, on his way to visit Russia with his staff and most of the ship's crew of 650 men, occurred on 5 June.
26. Later Lieut.-Col. A. F. A. N. Thorne, CMG, DSO.
27. News of the terrible losses on the Somme was evidently absorbed only gradually in the Ypres salient.
28. See Chapter 3 note 27 above.
29. 2/Lieut. E. C. Webster; see also diary for 16 September 1916.
30. His promotion to lieutenant was backdated, but it seems odd that news of it should have come from Lockeridge.
31. See diary for 31 October 1916.
32. A subsection was usually a single gun, with its limber and ammunition, the detachment constituting a sergeant's command.
33. Trones Wood, with Delville Wood, was among the most hotly contested features in this second phase of the Somme battle.
34. The Royal Munsters and other Irish regiments brigaded with them; the Dublin Fusiliers and the Irish Rifles distinguished themselves in the fighting round Guillemont and Ginchy. See also next two diary entries.

241

35. See note 33 above.
36. The assault on 15 September was the first use in action anywhere of this new weapon. Eddie, hard at work throughout these days, had time to notice it, but was evidently not expecting it to produce a decisive breakthrough.
37. The corps commander was presumably Lord Cavan.
38. The Guards Division memorial is by the road between these two places.
39. Lieutenant, later Major, G. F. Foley is often mentioned; see especially diary for 20 May and 20 August 1918.
40. The 'brown' line was a type of operational designation constantly in use. This was the line of objectives in the second phase of the Somme battle, the objectives in the third phase were designated the purple line.
41. The 6th Division had worked closely with the Guards Division, for example in the recent assault on Les Boeufs.

Chapter 5: Eddie's Diary: The Third Notebook

1. Lieut.-Col. F. A. Buzzard, DSO, was to command 74th Brigade, RFA from mid-November 1916 until late July 1917, and had previously commanded 61st Brigade. He gives Eddie dinner in Amiens on 14 November, and seems to have considered asking for him as his ADC, see diary for 14 December 1916.
2. Major A. S. Archdale, DSO, became brigade major, RA, from February 1917 to June 1918. In command of B Battery, 75th Brigade, RFA, when Eddie joined it, and later of B Battery, 61st Brigade. See also diary for 13 November 1916.
3. See diary for 4 August 1916 in Chapter 4.
4. See report by CO 7th Lincolns reproduced in diary after Eddie's leave from 16–26 November 1916.
5. See illustration of the gateway to the farm attached to the chateau taken in 1996. The chateau itself has been demolished.
6. Brigadier General W. Evans, DSO, was in command of the Guards Division artillery from March 1916, when he succeeded Brigadier General Wardrop until late May 1917.
7. This may be Captain H. S. MacDonald, who was in command of A Battery, 61 Brigade, RFA, in May 1916.
8. Godfects was a famous restaurant.
9. See note 1 above for 11 October diary.
10. See diary entry for 6 November 1916.
11. See diary for 22 January 1917.
12. Lieut. J. Williams, MC, often mentioned in the diary, was evidently

one of Eddie's closest friends. He was a section commander in B Battery, 75th Brigade, until wounded at Mory Copse on 27 August 1918.

13. See note 1 above for 11 October diary.
14. Major Grier was probably Major E. B. Greer, MC.
15. For Byrne, see diaries for 24 January and 7 March 1917.
16. See also diary for 20 August 1918.
17. See diary for 21 January 1918.
18. Major Reid, 127 Battery, had been in the retreat from Mons in 1914, in 29th Brigade, RFA, and had done well to get away without loss after the fighting at Le Cateau.
19. The 29th Division had come from Egypt and the Dardanelles, and included the battery Eddie's brother Sydney had commanded briefly before he was killed in action. See Appendix.
20. CO 4th Grenadier Guards, Lieut.-Col. G. C. Hamilton, DSO, later CMG.
21. He seems likely to have been 2/Lieut. F. J. Watts, who was killed in action on 17 July 1917.
22. Serre, on the plateau above the Ancre, was a key objective.
23. They were to advance towards Bullecourt.
24. It took a few days for this news to arrive.
25. Major E. N. E. M. Vaughan, DSO.
26. For the award of his Croix de Guerre, with which he is formally presented on 17 February, see diary.
27. The British were now fighting on both banks of the Ancre.
28. CO 2nd Grenadier Guards and later Brigadier General C. R. de Crespigny, CB, CMG, DSO. See Jack Giffard's diary for 1 September 1914, which reports the death in action of Lieut. C. H. Champion de Crespigny, 2nd Dragoon Guards, the Queen's Bays.
29. His promotion to acting captain, of which Eddie 'hears' again on 3 March (see diary) was dated from 18 February.
30. Perhaps 2/Lieut. G. E. L. Hancock.
31. Probably Lieut. S. G. M. David, MC, who was signal officer at 75th Brigade headquarters in 1918.
32. See also diary for 22 September 1917, where he is among Eddie's visitors in No. 4 casualty clearing station; this seems likely to have been 2/Lt. Porter, killed in action on 24 March 1918.
33. The Union flag first flew from the citadel on 11 March. Good news travels fast this time.
34. The diary has mentioned mud and rain repeatedly. Nevertheless, the British guns harried this major German withdrawal. At times, teams to draw the 18-pounders through the mire were increased to eight instead of the normal six horses.

35. See diary for 12 March 1916 and Chapter 4 note 8.
36. The diary later reports Major Corbett wounded on 12 April and killed by a sniper on 5 May 1918. He had been awarded the MC in August 1916 when captain in command of B Battery, 75th Brigade.
37. The United States' declaration of war on Germany dated from the President's address to Congress on 2 April.
38. The B25 aircraft type was probably a Sopwith two-seater.
39. The records consulted do not give this name. There was a distinguished pilot named Barkell who came from New South Wales.
40. On Feilding, see diary for 28 February 1916 and Chapter 4 note 5.
41. The Vimy offensive, in which the Canadians earned such distinction, had been launched only that morning, early.
42. Thess offensives, which occurred on 14 April, as in the diary for 9 and 10 April, took place in the area of Vimy Ridge.
43. This French success was to the north of the Aisne, towards the Chemin des Dames; also beyond Rheims, round Auberive. It did not lift morale in the French army. General Nivelle, so recently praised for his leadership at Verdun, was publicly criticized, and retired.
44. Major-General the Earl of Cavan, KP, later Field Marshal, GCMG, GCVO, KCB, had commanded the 4th Guards Brigade in 1914, and the Guards Division from June 1915, before General Feilding. He became GOC XIV Corps in January 1916, leaving them at the time of 3rd Ypres to take over as C-in-C in Italy later in 1917.
45. Major-General J. Ponsonby, CMG, DSO, later CB, became a divisional commander in 1917. One of his brothers was Keeper of the Privy Purse at Buckingham Palace; another was an MP.
46. HRH The Prince of Wales had been commissioned in the Grenadiers early in the war and appointed to French's staff: later, he paid a number of visits to the front, as did HM King George V.
47. An NCT is a propellent for the 18-pounders (nitro-cellulose, tubular).
48. GOCRA of 4th Army was Major-General C. E. D. Budworth.
49. Up north meant Ypres.
50. The political situation had been deteriorating fast for many months, from long before Milner's visit in February of that year, but was not well understood in Allied capitals let alone by officers on the Western Front.
51. The Italians' success was either in the Plava area generally or in the taking of Hill 652.
52. More than two weeks' notice at battery level of the major Messines offensive might seem surprising, but was surely inevitable given the forward position assigned to their guns, as noted in the diary for 26 May.

53. This may refer to Staff Sergeant A. Skull of D Battery who was wounded on 23 August 1918 at Hamelincourt.

54. The attack on Messines Ridge and Wytschaete followed the greatest mining operation in the war. It was successful in relieving the pressure on the Ypres salient by securing valuable high ground and depriving the enemy of advantages he had long enjoyed. Eddie's battery did well to suffer comparatively light casualties, see diary for 10 June.

55. Gamble was presumably his soldier servant. Eddie later hears that Gamble has been wounded, see diary for 8 December 1917.

56. Perhaps from battery headquarters. Kane seems to have become Eddie's batman, see diary for 5 November 1918.

57. There seems to have been a bit of a conspiracy to get Eddie off on this fourth leave without his having had formally to report sick.

58. Waddell was later second in command and successor to Eddie in A Battery, 75th Brigade RFA. See concluding notes.

Chapter 6: Eddie's Diary: The Fourth Notebook

1. One of the earliest severe raids on London by the Gotha aircraft, causing heavy casualties.

2. For Davies, see diary for 18 December 1917 and 21 February 1918.

3. Perhaps an echo of the last organized pre-revolutionary Russian offensive towards Lvov, in the latter part of June, which ended in disintegration, desertion and disaster.

4. See Chapter 5 note 58.

5. Two British battalions holding a small bridgehead east of the Yser had been overwhelmed by a massive German attack.

6. Probably Lieut. K. M. McCracken.

7. Wartime usage, perhaps originating as an aid to deliberately casual understatement.

8. See diary for 6 September when he gets 'a nice blighty'. Lieut. W. R. Seward was on duty at Headquarters 75th Brigade, RFA, on 11 November 1918.

9. Captain G. W. McFadyean, MC, was adjutant at Headquarters 75th Brigade, RFA, at the close of hostilities.

10. This might suggest that Major Hovil has resumed command of the battery, which had fallen to Eddie on 16 July. See diary for that date, but see also note 13 below.

11. See note 7 above.

12. This was the opening of the third battle of Ypres, in which the salient was gradually expanded. French troops to the north, on the left of the Guards Division, crossed the Yser Canal to take

Steenstraate and move on towards Bixschoote. The Guards Division then crossed the canal to move on Pilkem and drive towards Langemarck, with a Welsh division on their right. It rained incessantly until 6 August.

13. Those named, with Eddie himself, look like the commanders for the time being of each of the batteries in the 75th Brigade, so perhaps Hovil was still commanding the brigade. The diary does not make clear when Eddie relinquished his temporary command. See his diary for 24 July 1917.

14. Some of the officers in 74th Brigade reported as killed in action and wounded have been mentioned before in the diary. See also the letter reproduced before the diary entry for 26 November 1916, which is countersigned by Lieut. H. Vaughan, as Adjutant, 61st Brigade, RFA.

15. For Major Corbett, see diary for 31 March 1917 and for 12 April and 5 May 1918.

16. See diary for 18 September 1917 and passim. Seigne was major in command of C Battery, 75th Brigade, RFA, at the end of the war.

17. Fourche Farm and all the other features mentioned in the diary from now until Eddie is wounded on 29 September are to be found in all the detailed accounts and maps of the fighting round Ypres at this time.

18. For F subsection dugout, see Chapter 4, note 32.

19. In the second phase of the third battle of Ypres, Irish regiments fighting in the central sector of the salient, to the south of the Guards Division, suffered a serious reverse.

20. Major A. Z. Blumenthal.

21. Lieut.-Col. G. B. S. Follett, DSO, MVO, died 1918.

22. See note 8 above.

23. Lieut. J. L. Edwards had been at Headquarters, 61st Brigade, in 1916, and earlier with Y Guards trench mortar battery. 2/Lieut. G. P. Jenkins, RA, had joined Eddie's brigade more recently.

24. SOS meant ready to bring down a defensive curtain of artillery fire on prearranged lines if requested by a sector of the front trenches under enemy attack. See diary for 16 September 1917.

25. See Chapter 4 note 32.

26. Captain H. M. Cockcroft, MC, was medical officer to 75th Brigade RFA until the end of the war.

27. His friends from the battery were able to visit him in the casualty clearing station because he had been wounded when they were on the point of going out of the line to rest.

28. A copy of a letter of 12 October from Colonel Bethell is reproduced in the diary, after the entry for 25 September. Colonel A. B. Bethell,

DSO, was in command of 75th Brigade RFA from October 1915 until mid-March 1918.

29. One of the earliest night raids on London, in which some 17 Gotha aircraft took part.
30. Maudie, his youngest sister, was nursing in a London hospital.
31. Lieut.-Col. S. Stallard, CBE, DSO.
32. May, who was three years younger than he was and the sister closest to Eddie in age, served as a nurse in the VAD both in France and in Palestine, and was mentioned in dispatches; later, Mrs. W. I. Cheesman.
33. Lieut.-Col. J. H. M. Arden, DSO.
34. Lord Ailesbury was a country neighbour at Tottenham House in Savernake Forest of Eddie's father, and served with him as a magistrate on the bench at Marlborough; he was currently with the Guards Division. A letter from him on the occasion of Eddie's death survived in the Lockeridge papers. Until some time in the 1930s, Lord Ailesbury would come into Marlborough in a 1908 Trojan motorcar with solid tyres and park outside the Ailesbury Arms. He lived latterly in the Channel Islands. His son, then Lord Cardigan, was captured by the Germans at the time of Dunkirk, in 1940, escaped and made his way, mostly on foot, to Spain, as recorded in his first book, *I Walked by Night*.
35. This must refer to the famous counterattack by the Guards Division at Gouzeaucourt.
36. See diary for 4 and 5 March and 30 March 1918, when Panton is reported wounded.
37. Gamble was at one time Eddie's batman, see diary for 16 June 1917 and Chapter 5 note 55.
38. Probably Lieut. A. Livingstone, RA.
39. Almost certainly Captain F. J. Okell, who appreciated highly Eddie's support for him in his work as Church of England chaplain to 75th Brigade RFA.
40. See W. E. Giffard's diary for this day, 11 December 1917, and Chapter 8 note 9.
41. Jerusalem was surrendered on 7 December. Allenby (then General) entered the city formally on 9 December.
42. The *mairie* at Habarcq may well look much as it did then, see illustration on p. 145.
43. Captain T. A. M. Finch was veterinary officer at brigade headquarters.
44. Eddie's spelling of such names is unreliable. This is probably T. F. H. Read, who ended the war as lieutenant in command of a section of C Battery, 75th Brigade.

45. Young Arnold-Forster was from Wroughton, near Swindon. Two members of the family were gunners, while M. N. Arnold-Forster was a lieutenant in the Grenadier Guards.
46. John Willie was Lieut. J. Williams, MC. To judge from the diary, he was probably Eddie's closest friend at this period of the war.
47. See diary for 6 April 1918 for report of his death.
48. Lieutenant D. McCorquordale.
49. Frequently mentioned in the diary, Captain J. J. Emberton, MC, was second in command of C Battery on 11 November 1918.
50. Wyatt was often mentioned. Lieut. O. E. P. Wyatt, MC, was a section commander in C Battery on 11 November.
51. Sutton-Nelthorpe was probably a contemporary at Horris Hill Preparatory School. If this was Oliver Sutton-Nelthorpe, he was later Lieutenant-Colonel, DSO, MC.
52. This was a battery commanders' course.
53. Captain T. Hussey, RA, is not mentioned again.
54. Davies was mentioned on 11 July and 18 December 1917.
55. 2/Lieut. B. H. B. Stockton, MC was a section commander in Eddie's battery at the end.
56. Eddie's sister Cicely's brother-in-law, Lieut.-Col. G. K. Maurice, DSO, MC, one of the youngest of 11 brothers, who served in the RAMC in both world wars, and in the Sudan during much of the interwar period. See *The Marlborough Doctors* by T. R. Maurice.
57. 'E & Y' hut was evidently a sort of predecessor of the NAAFI; it provided some respite close to the front.
58. The 135th Battery RFA had distinguished themselves at Le Cateau, in the retreat from Mons, and since.
59. The great German offensive of March and April 1918 was evidently not unexpected in the sector round Arras.
60. Aubrey Wade vividly reports what happened to the 5th Army, as experienced by a battery of field artillery, in *Gunner on the Western Front*.
61. Perhaps Lieut. E. M. Ellis, MC, killed in action on 7 August 1918.
62. See diary for 7 December 1917 and for Major Senior's death, see diary for 15 April 1918.
63. 2/Lieut. W. H. A. F. Panton.
64. Captain J. A. Radford, MC. See also diary for 29 May and 24 June 1918.
65. Captain W. H. Henshaw was a section commander and later second in command of A Battery.
66. Lieut.-Col. J. B. Riddell, DSO, formerly in command of 74th Brigade RFA from May to November 1916, had taken over at 75th Brigade from Colonel Bethell only one week before he was

248

wounded. He was succeeded by Lieut.-Col. W. C. E. Rudkin, CMG, DSO, who remained with them until 24 June.

67. For McFadzean, see note 9 above for 20 July 1917.

68. Moriarty and Mullen both seem to have been posted away from the brigade, Lieut. G. H. Moriarty to a staff appointment.

69. See note 44 above.

70. The 25th RF was a battalion of the Royal Fusiliers.

71. Captain L. S. Campbell, MC, was second in command of D Battery when wounded at Boursies on 26 September, perhaps assumed command temporarily, see note 73 below.

72. Lieut. Cropper had been in D Battery, 75th Brigade, mentioned in the *Brigade War Diary* as having entered the German front line with an infantry patrol on 14 March 1918 and 'found it unoccupied'.

73. Major E. J. T. Housden, MC, commanded D Battery until wounded on 8 September at Boursies.

74. On Lieut.-Col. W. C. E. Rudkin, see note 66 above.

75. Bird and Eddie meet again at a casualty clearing station on 14 October. This was probably Captain D. Bird, MC.

76. Major L. Holt, MC, commanded A Battery until 23 August, when he was wounded at Boiry St Martin, and succeeded by Eddie.

77. The doctor was probably Captain H. M. Cockcroft, MC, see also note 26 above.

78. See note 65 above.

79. Maud Giffard recorded that Foley joined the family party to see Eddie off at Victoria station after the latter's last home leave. He later wrote of his admiration for Eddie's professionalism and 'willing endurance'.

Chapter 7: Eddie's Diary: The Fifth Notebook

1. There had been a week of good weather already.

2. For Emberton, see Chapter 6 note 49, and later diary passim.

3. This was probably Major H. B. Dresser, DSO, who was in command of B Battery when wounded at Boiry St Martin on 21 August 1918. See also diary for 15 June.

4. Captain T. A. M. Finch was veterinary officer at 75th Brigade headquarters.

5. For Hancock, see diary for 7 March 1917 and Chapter 5 note 30.

6. For Henshaw, see Chapter 6 note 65 for entry of 31 March 1918, and diary passim.

7. For Wyatt, see Chapter 6 note 50 for diary of 17 March 1918, and later diary passim.

8. For Radford, see Chapter 6 note 64 for 30 March 1918, and later diary passim.

9. For Finch, see note 4 above and later diary passim.

10. Lieut.-Col. C. E. Vickery, DSO, had been in command of 74th Brigade RFA since late July 1917.

11. The anti-tank gun was a new requirement, first noted in the diary on 4 May 1918.

12. Major L. Holt, MC, was in command of A Battery when he was wounded at Boiry St Martin on 23 August.

13. Brigadier General F. A. Wilson, CMG, DSO, was about to take over command of Guards Division artillery from Brigadier General Evans. See also diary for 17 June 1918.

14. 24th Battalion Royal Fusiliers. See also diary for 17 April 1918.

15. Major P. G. Yorke was Brigade Major, RA, from 24 June to 10 October 1918.

16. Could WSCE be 'Wine, Sacramental, Church of England for the use of'?

17. For Read, see Chapter 6 note 44 for diary entry on 20 December 1917, and diary passim.

18. Contrast this French advance with diary for 31 May. The German army was now beginning to retreat all along the Western Front, the great offensives of the spring exhausted and reversed. This is apparent in the diary for Eddie's own sector of the front; see also for example diary for 8 August and 13 September.

19. For Moriarty, see Chapter 6 note 68.

20. Perhaps this was a farewell dinner for Colonel Rudkin, see diary for 26 August 1918.

21. Major E. P. Dawson was in command of D Battery, 75th Brigade, RFA, at the end of the war.

22. Eddie's sister Maud noted that Major Foley, who was still convalescent (see diary for 20 May 1918 and Chapter 6 note 79), was among those who saw him off.

23. Bobbie was the elder son of Eddie's late sister Violet and Oliver Maurice. See also Chapter 9 note 2.

24. Captain A. A. B. Hay, MC. See also diary for 1 January 1917.

25. Captain J. A. Gascoigne Cecil was to be killed in action at Mory Copse on 27 August (q.v.).

26. The gunners, without all the drivers, artificers and others not directly involved in serving the guns.

27. Lieut.-Col. T. Kirkland, DSO, had taken over command of 75th Brigade RFA from Colonel Rudkin in late June.

28. See note 25 above.

29. Lieut. J. Williams, MC, a close friend of Eddie's (see diary passim), had not rejoined B Battery by the end of hostilities.

30. For Godfrey, see diary for 25 February 1918 and Chapter 6 note 56.
31. 2/Lieut. J. A. Howfield, MC, was killed in action at Ecoust.
32. See also diary for 24 August and 6 September 1918.
33. 2/Lieut. A. Downing, perhaps just joined, was with B Battery on 11 November 1918.
34. Major T. R. B. Seigne, MC, and Lieut. T. F. H. Read, both wounded at Louverval on this day, were both on duty on 11 November.
35. 2/Lieut. H. McD. Paterson of B Battery had been wounded at Boursies on 8 September.
36. Captain W. E. Phipps had succeeded Captain Finch as Army Veterinary Corps officer at 75th Brigade headquarters.
37. This was Lieut. A. M. W. Napier. See also diary for 15 September; he had been killed in action at Demicourt on 12 September.
38. 2/Lieut. J. St C. Lindsay was with C Battery on 11 November.
39. Major L. Holt, MC, had already been wounded at Boiry St Martin on 23 August. Captain Henshaw took over A Battery until Eddie assumed its command on 10 October.
40. Victory at Megiddo was effectively the conclusion of General Allenby's campaign, see diary for 4 October.
41. These crossings were of the Canal du Nord.
42. See note 40 above.
43. Drivers G. Baskeyfield and J. Ferguson of C Battery were killed in action at Rumilly.
44. The chateau at Lesdain, even if not as well kept as now, may have provided Eddie with a comfortable night, of a quality not to be repeated, except perhaps at Haussy (see diary for 24 October).
45. 2/Lieut. W. A. C. Grantham was wounded two days later, see diary, between Quievy and au-Tertre Farm, at the same time as Eddie.
46. The Shop refers to the Royal Military Academy Woolwich where all gunner and sapper officers were trained for the regular army.
47. The farm is properly named Ferme de Fontaine-au-Tertre and, as in 1918, it still belongs to the Aublin family.
48. 2/Lieut. C. J. Dartnall was a section commander in A Battery.
49. These were dressing stations set up by the officer commanding the 3rd Field Ambulance, who gave Eddie a good night before sending him to the two casualty clearing stations, further back, see diary.
50. For Bird, see also diary for 18 October 1918, 1 May 1918, and Chapter 6 note 75.
51. Lieut. K. R. Hughes was reported wounded on 14 October at Nine Wood. He was in A Battery.
52. For Stockton, see note 63 below.
53. 2/Lieut. C. J. Dartnall was a section commander in A Battery.
54. Major R. Darley, MC, had taken over command of B Battery.

55. 2/Lieut. E. F. Holloway was wounded at au-Tertre Farm.

56. It seems that Sergeant Tetley's wound may not have kept him out of action.

57. The Revd F. W. Head, MC, had followed Pat McCormick (see diary for 12 March 1916, and Chapter 4 note 8) as senior Church of England chaplain to the forces, Guards Division.

58. At Villers-Pol Eddie's advance crossed Jack Giffard's line of retreat in 1914. There is a plaque on the outer wall of the church inscribed '*La Société des anciens Combatants a leur Camarades anglais.*'

59. 2/Lieut. A. T. Abley had been with A Battery since before Colonel Kirkland took over 75th Brigade.

60. Kane was Eddie's batman, see also diary for 19 June 1917 and Chapter 5 note 56.

61. Drivers W. Needham and R. A. Rowles of A Battery were among those wounded at La Longueville that day.

62. Eddie took over from his second in command, Captain J. G. Waddell, who resumed command after Eddie was hit the following day. Waddell, who had himself been wounded as recently as 1 September, at L'Homme Mort, has been a familiar figure in the diary. He took the battery on into Germany after the Armistice. He wrote several times to Eddie's father and sister Maud. He visited them later at Lockeridge House, bringing with him the cartridge case of the last shell fired by A Battery, still under Eddie's command, before the cessation of hostilities.

63. Eddie was presumably hit very soon after making this last optimistic entry in his diary. He died of his wounds on 10 November. The shell that knocked him out on 8 November also wounded two other officers of A Battery, 2/Lieut. M. Hall, MM, and 2/Lieut. B. H. B. Stockton, MC, the latter only lightly. They were sharing a bivouac near Les Mottes Farm. The farm is still in good order, eighty odd years on. The shell was said to have been one of the last three fired by the German guns in this sector. See also the final paragraph of the notes to Walter Giffard's diary, on the letter of 15 November 1918, in which he wrote of his talk with the sister who had looked after Eddie and Hall in the casualty clearing station close to what is now Awoingt British Cemetery, near Cambrai. There, Major Edmund Hamilton Giffard's grave is in Plot III, Row D, No. 6.

Chapter 8: *Walter's Diary: The First Notebook*

1. Unlike Eddie, Walter does not record who saw him off at Victoria station; we may be sure that some members of the family were there.

NOTES

2. Bairnsfather, the famous ('if you know a better 'ole') cartoonist.

3. Tony Allback, as it seems from the records, was Walter's exact contemporary in the Royal Flying Corps.

4. The Wing was commanded by Lieut.-Col. W. F. MacNeece, DSO.

5. Usually known as 13th KBS (Kite Balloon Section).

6. Swan Chateau was perhaps the Behagel family's house in the woods on the left of the road from Bailleul to Loker, under Mont Rouge.

7. Archie was anti-aircraft guns and gunfire.

8. This Scouting Experimental biplane, made in the Royal Aircraft Factory, came into service in the spring of 1917.

9. This was the day on which Eddie's diary (q.v.) recorded that he had heard from Walter 'who was near Ypres'.

10. Olantigh was the Loudon family's house in Kent where Walter had greatly enjoyed invitations to shoot and play tennis while he was studying at Wye Agricultural College and waiting to be accepted by the RFC.

11. See Introduction and Eddie's diary for 14 April 1916. Bob was Jack Giffard's twin brother. He was a field gunner and had been promoted captain to serve as ADC to Major General S. H. Lomax, commanding the First Division. He died of wounds received the previous day, on 1 November 1914. His grave is in the town cemetery at Ypres (Row E1, Grave 12).

12. A wind of up to about 50 miles per hour was regarded as acceptable for operations. 13th KBS would have been using French balloons of the Drachen type, but see diary for 8 January 1918.

13. No. 9 was 9th KBS. There were two sections to a company and two companies to a wing.

14. Or Droogland.

15. A battery of 330 Brigade, RFA.

16. Hunter was perhaps the company commander. Stories about pretending to be an officer of that name on the telephone and finding that he was unexpectedly at the other end of the line were current years later.

17. Surely he means 2.00 a.m.

18. See Eddie's diary for 9 January 1918 and 20 January 1918. It was a battery commanders' course at Shoebury and Salisbury.

19. Maximum height on a very calm day might have been about 6000 feet, but operational heights were usually well below that. The strain on the cable was a crucial factor, as the diary makes clear. See also, for example, diary of 2 April 1918.

20. Going south usually meant to the Somme.

21. This was Walter's 22nd birthday.

22. Jenny was his brother Bob's widow and mother of Robina. See last paragraph of Chapter 7 and Chapter 4 note 1.

23. The abbreviation 'dis' for 'disconnected' was standard Great War slang.
24. Alcock was perhaps a nickname for Allback (Tony), who reappears after Walter's leave. Three days before his time fits with quarterly leave: they had embarked for the front on 5 December 1917.
25. X 3 referred to the 3rd KBS.
26. The Bath road, the road from Marlborough to Bath, later the A4, passes close to Lockeridge and was the highway by the standards of which the family judged all others.
27. The shoulder support was an essential component in the fitting of Walter's artificial leg.

Chapter 9: Walter's Diary: The Second Notebook

1. Again, there is no mention of who saw him off at Victoria station. Walter is evidently fully aware of the great importance of the German offensive that had begun on the Somme on 21 March. See Eddie's diary for that day.
2. Jackie was the younger son of Walter's eldest sister, Violet and his godfather 'Tiny' Maurice. Orphaned very young, Jackie and his brother Bobbie were brought up thereafter at Lockeridge House, 'Dud' and his sister-in-law, Laura Hamilton, sharing the responsibility. Jackie became a regular soldier and went to France in 1939 as adjutant in the East Surreys. He returned to France on 'D' Day in 1944, in command of the second battalion of the King's Shropshire Light Infantry, and was awarded the DSO. He was killed a month after the landing, and his grave is in one of the smaller Normandy cemeteries maintained by the Commonwealth War Graves Commission. See *The History of the Second Battalion, 1944–45* by Major G. L. Y. Radcliffe, assisted by Captain R. Sale (Oxford: Blackwell, 1947).
3. The gas tubes were long metal cylinders of hydrogen with which to fill the balloon.
4. Laycock was presumably their company commander. See also 11 April 1918 diary entry.
5. They were awarded observers' wings in the form of an oval shield, with RFC embroidered on it, and one wing, in cloth, to be sewn onto the tunic above the left-hand breast pocket.
6. During the last three weeks or so before Walter's second home leave, it is clear that there was a concerted effort to persuade him to put in for a recording officer's appointment. It may be that he accepted this and that the result was the easier circumstances that had little, he thought, worth putting into a continued diary. This would be consistent with his remark at the beginning of the second notebook.

7. He was promoted captain (acting/temporary), so it seems possible that he became a company commander. He celebrated the end of the Great War at a restaurant in Brussels, but the celebration was blighted. A letter home survives in which Walter reported a visit to the casualty clearing station where Eddie had died. This letter was dated 15 November. Walter reported that he had seen the sister who had nursed Eddie, and how they had had to operate as soon as he was brought in: also how one of his subalterns, Hall, wounded at the same time, had spoken continually of the whole battery's devotion to Eddie and admiration for him. The letter said that Eddie's grave was in an entirely British cemetery 'outside the CCS, with just a simple wooden cross.' This is now Awoingt British Cemetery, near Cambrai, and the stone memorial is at Plot III, Row D, Grave 6.

Index